THE WORLD'S WEIRDEST SPORTS

Bog snorkelling, dwile flonking, goat grabbing and more...

PAUL CONNOLLY

PIER 9

Contents

Introduction

When first considering an appropriate title for this book, I was keen for it to embrace and reflect everything within these pages. Yet my initial suggestion, *Bog Snorkelling, Goat Grabbing, Dwile Flonking: Some of the World's More Obscure Sports, Games, Pastimes and Assorted Harebrained Activities that the Aforementioned Sports, Games and Pastimes Will No Doubt be Embarrassed to be Associated With*, was accurate enough but, as I was told by someone more attuned to matters of marketing, not quite what the publisher was looking for. 'We love what you're trying to say but it might just be a tad too long, a touch too convoluted,' they said. 'On that, you do realize that you don't get paid by the word, right?'

After going through my contract and discovering I was indeed writing under a false impression, we were left with the title you have already seen stamped emphatically on the cover. While *The World's Weirdest Sports* has the brevity and snap necessary to leap out and accost book buyers it does, I'm not too proud to concede, have its imperfections, one of which is the use of the definite article, which suggests the following pages list every single one of the world's weirdest sports, which, of course, they don't. Fans of greased piglet chasing, for instance, will note the omission of their beloved pastime, which narrowly failed to make the cut. Chasing a slick little piggy around a muddy enclosure is, I've no doubt, a wonderfully fulfilling pursuit, but a line had to be drawn somewhere.

That (or rather, 'The') aside, my biggest concern with this book's title is with the use of the words 'weirdest' and 'sports'. 'Weirdest', for one, prompts the question, 'Weird in comparison to what?' Tom Cruise, for example, may be weird to some, quite possibly even his own parents. But is he weird in comparison to Michael Jackson? Is anyone weird in comparison to Michael Jackson? Who or what is the control group or standard of normality when it comes to judging weirdness? Simply, there isn't one. Weirdness is a purely subjective measure. Thus, throwing dried-up chips of cow manure (see page 98) may appear weird to some, but is it really any weirder than the significantly more popular game of cricket, a complex sport of laws and by-laws that is played in trousers and can last 5 days and still not produce a winner?

Reduce any sport to its bare elements and objectives and the most basic question an outsider might ask—'Why do you do it?'—has only one real answer, particularly when you exclude all the other answers an articulate person might come up with (such as 'for fun', 'to get fit', 'to push myself physically and emotionally' and 'because my wife wants me out of the house at least for a few hours every weekend'). 'Because. Just because.' To some, that defines the beauty of sport; the playing for playing's sake. To others, particularly those who never have an inclination, let alone an instinct, to turn to the sports pages first, that's about as weird as it gets.

As for the use of the word 'sport', well, that's a noun that usually describes an activity requiring physical exertion and skill. One could argue that such a definition excludes the likes of accepted sports such as golf and lawn bowls, let alone some of the so-called sports found within this book, such as conkers, rock paper scissors, sauna sitting and *tejo*, which, you'll discover, is a Colombian sport similar to quoits but with explosives. It should be noted, however, that an archaic definition of sport describes it as anything that is a source of amusement and entertainment. If that generous definition stops any sticklers out there from getting a little knotted up in the knicker department when they see sauna sitting listed as a sport, then well and good.

To put it simply, for the sake of titular brevity and in order to accommodate, under as few descriptors as possible, an unrelated, eclectic mix of recreational activities, we have stretched the definition of 'weirdest' and 'sports' further than a retired footballer's waistband. I hope you accept this in the good humour in which I've attempted to write this book—for if humour has no place within sporting endeavour then, to my mind, sport, at any level, isn't worth a damn.

For most people arm wrestling is like karaoke; something they rarely do sober. For others it is the kind of contest they left behind in childhood when their father would condescend to arm wrestle them before feigning a struggle and submitting with an embarrassingly exaggerated groan that brought to mind a distressed brontosaurus. However, to its devotees—men and women with forearms like Christmas hams—arm wrestling is a serious sport demanding rigorous training and even tactical acumen. In countries like Australia, Canada, England and the United States there are governing bodies, regular tournaments, weight divisions, and specialized equipment for competition[1] and training.

---

1 A purpose-built arm-wrestling table is used in official competitions. It has two cushions on which the competitors place their respective elbows, another two cushions on each side of the mid line (onto which one competitor hopes to pin the other's hand) and two stabilizing bars that each wrestler is allowed to hold

At first glance, arm wrestling is a simple sport. Two people—perhaps looking for something to prove, or just a way to hold hands without attracting undue attention—face each other and place their right (or left) elbows on a table. They then lock thumbs, clasp each other's hand and attempt to force it down onto the table—without lifting their respective elbows—by pushing their opponent's hand backwards. Depending on the relative strength of the two competitors, this could take a fraction of a second, a few minutes, or longer.

An arm wrestler's best asset is obviously the strength of his bicep and forearm—which, to digress, would make Popeye near unbeatable (although the appropriate authorities might have to consider whether or not spinach is a performance-enhancing substance and thus banned). To anyone who's ever witnessed an arm-wrestling tournament it may seem that only brute force, a goatee and a lifetime's over-consumption of red meat is required to be a successful arm wrestler, but other factors have an influence, such as hand size, finger strength and arm flexibility, which can allow an arm wrestler to maintain sufficient force despite his arm being pushed backwards at a disconcerting angle.

Wrestling technique and tactics are also important at a competitive level, and top wrestlers are known to have speciality moves. One popular move, known as 'the hook', is considered an 'inside' move because a wrestler is attempting to overpower an opponent's arm instead of his hand. To perform the hook, an arm wrestler curls his wrist as hard as he can and turns his fist towards his body. At the same time, he positions his body over his arm—as close to it as possible without touching—so he can use his arm and body weight to pin his opponent. With most of the contact at the point of the wrist he effectively takes his opponent's hand out of the match.

----

onto with his non-wrestling hand. Reflecting the seriousness of elite competition, an arm-wrestling table has no beer-glass holders or peanut receptacles.

Another key move, an 'outside' move, is the 'top roll', in which a competitor rolls his wrist forward, thereby bending back his opponent's hand towards his wrist, thus compromising his opponent's leverage. While exerting as much downward pressure on his opponent's hand (he can effectively lean off the table as long as his wrestling elbow remains in place), he then slowly attempts to walk his fingers higher on his opponent's hand, thus improving his own leverage and chances of victory.

While the origins of arm wrestling are unknown (it has variously been linked to the ancient Egyptians, the Native Americans and Snoopy [2]), its future appears limitless now that computers can communicate the sense of touch. Boffins at the New York Hall of Science, seemingly with nothing better to do, have recently made the world's first internet arm-wrestling machine, which allows two people on opposite sides of a room—or opposite sides of the world—to arm wrestle each other. A computer interprets the movement and power of a person pushing a lever in Place A then sends that interpretation to another computer, which creates the appropriate level of resistance on another lever in Place B.

Viewed optimistically, this important breakthrough in arm-wrestling technology could be the answer to non-violent conflict negotiation the world has been looking for. Or perhaps not …

----

2 In 1968, *Peanuts* creator Charles Schultz drew a series of widely distributed comic strips in which his world-famous beagle, Snoopy, was working towards competing in the so-called World Wristwrestling Championships in Petaluma, California. Sadly, Snoopy was eliminated from the tournament before it started because the championship rules stated that a competitor must lock thumbs with his opponent. And Snoopy, of course, had no thumbs. While Snoopy's dream was shattered, the publicity his storyline gave the sport of arm wrestling was priceless. In 1969, American network ABC's *Wide World of Sports* program televised the world championships from Petaluma, the home of organized arm wrestling in the United States.

Another form of wrestling

Since 1994, toe wrestling has been an annual event at Ye Olde Royal Oak (Inn) in Wetton, Staffordshire, England. Competitors sit facing each other on the floor and extend their right (or left) foot towards each other while keeping their heels on their own side of a specially made toe rack. They then link big toes. When the bout starts with a cry of 'Toes away!' they attempt to push their opponent's foot over until it touches one of the wooden brackets set up on each side of the toe rack.

As suggested by the event's slogan ('There's no 'arm in it'), the World Toe Wrestling Championships are as much an opportunity for toe-related puns as anything else. Consider that a warning for what follows. Should a competitor wish to surrender during a bout, they must shout 'Toe much!'; the wrestling stage is called the 'toe-dium'; and bouts are referred to as 'toe-downs'. Even wrestlers get in on the act, with one recent competitor referring to himself as the Toe-minator. As Snoopy's long-suffering companion, Charlie Brown, might say: 'Good grief!'.

BASE Jumping

It could be said that an adrenaline, or extreme, activity is one in which the serious injury or death of a participant is a distinct possibility. And it could be further suggested that the more likely serious injury or death is—and the higher the participant's adrenaline levels inevitably rise as a result—the more exciting, in the broadest meaning of the word, the activity becomes. By such a definition, BASE jumping can't be too far behind running towards the White House while screaming obscenities and brandishing a meat cleaver as just about the most exciting extreme activity in the world.

An offshoot of skydiving, BASE jumping involves leaping off natural or human-made structures—such as cliff faces, bridges, skyscrapers and telecommunications towers—before deploying a parachute and, all going well, drifting safely to the ground. As such, it is far cheaper than skydiving (which requires jumpers to fork out for a one-way trip on a breezy aircraft); disregarding the cost of funerals should things go splat.

An acronym, 'BASE' stands for Building, Antennae, Span, Earth; all things you can jump off, should you be of a certain mind. It is commonly believed Carl Boenish, filmmaker and BASE jumper, coined the acronym in 1978[1] after he filmed four men jumping from the 975-metre El Capitan, a spectacular granite monolith in Yosemite National Park, California.[2] Since filming that jump, Boenish went on to develop and promote the sport and, consequently, is widely considered to be the father of modern BASE jumping. ('Modern' because there have been examples in the past of people using parachutes to dramatically descend from fixed objects. For example, in 1912 Frederick Law jumped from the Statue of Liberty in New York City.) Unfortunately, Boenish's paternal reign over BASE jumping ended in 1984 at an 1100-metre cliff face called the Trollveggen (Troll Wall) in Norway, when he died during a jump gone wrong.

Before this accident, however, Boenish oversaw the pursuit of a structured and new form of parachuting. Prior to this, BASE jumps were more like one-off

---

1 It's believed he first considered the acronym BEST (as in Base, Earth, Span, Tower) before settling on BASE. It's been suggested by critics with a black sense of humour that BASE could also stand for 'Bones and Shit Everywhere'.

2 Long a popular rock-climbing site, El Capitan was first used as a platform from which to jump in 1966, with the two men who made the leap both sustaining broken bones from pushing themselves away from the cliff face as they fell. In 1980, after a brief experimentation with permits, the National Park Service decided to ban BASE jumping from El Capitan, considering it to be too dangerous. In October 1999, BASE jumper and stuntwoman Jan Davis made an illegal BASE jump from El Capitan to protest against the ban. She died in the attempt—somewhat undermining her intended statement, one has to think. Compounding the tragedy, and the irony, Davis' jump was also intended as a memorial to Frank Gambalie III who had, a few months earlier, successfully completed a BASE jump from El Capitan, only to drown in the Merced River while trying to evade park rangers.

   What with a number of other BASE jumping deaths from El Capitan, the sport's relationship with Yosemite National Park remains rocky.

stunts. Boenish had the idea of using ram-air parachutes (long, rectangular chutes, as opposed to more customary round chutes) and technique that involves diving away from the object rather than merely jumping off it. Both the ram-air parachutes and the free-fall technique were, and are still, intended to give jumpers more control over speed and direction as they fall.

There can be no argument that BASE jumping is a dangerous sport, not least because the slightest error, human or mechanical, will probably lead to death (to some in the sport, this is a badge of honour). The same cannot be said of motor racing and rock climbing, two sports BASE jumpers often compare their sport to when attempting to downplay its inherent danger.

Figures are rubbery, but at least 110 people are thought to have been killed when BASE jumping. However, proponents of the sport believe authorities and the media—who are, to be fair, prone to the odd bout of hysteria—treat BASE jumping unfairly. Supporters believe that many other sports are equally dangerous yet are not subject to the same criticism. Indeed, proponents of throwing yourself off a cliff believe that if a BASE jumper is well trained, if she's aware of the peculiarities of a particular site, if she uses BASE-specific equipment, if she conducts the jump in the right weather conditions and if she makes a jump commensurate with her skill and experience, then the sport is relatively safe.[3] Which, of course, is a few too many 'ifs' for the sport's critics, who just can't seem to get around the fact that anyone would choose to throw herself off anything higher than a springboard at a swimming pool.

One of the many differences between skydiving and BASE jumping is the much lower altitude at which BASE jumps take place and, as a result, the lower speed with which jumpers travel—some may say plummet—towards the ground.

----

3 Relative to what, however, would be the question. One would assume that if you compared the safety of BASE jumping with that of, say, fly fishing, then BASE jumping would be relatively dangerous.

For example, a skydiver can free-fall at around 160 kilometres per hour before deploying her chute. If she plans to keep her dinner date that evening she'll release her chute at least 600 metres from the ground. But most BASE jumps are initiated below 600 metres, meaning a jumper's chute has to open quickly and soundly (with the jumper travelling at around 80 kilometres per hour) because, from 600 metres, a jumper will hit the ground in less than 6 seconds if not slowed by a parachute.

The main problem with falling at a lower speed is that it gives jumpers less control during free fall, which increases the likelihood they could tumble through the air. This, in turn, increases the likelihood of a deployed parachute malfunctioning and becoming tangled. Tumbling also means the jumper may not necessarily know where she is in relation to the object she has jumped off. And of course, after all that, even if a BASE jumper were able to quickly ascertain a problem, she would not have time before hitting the ground to deploy a reserve chute—which is why BASE jumpers don't carry one.

The ground, of course, is a major concern, since not all BASE jumping sites are surrounded by a vast, flat and soft landing site, like an ocean of foam rubber, for instance. Arguably of more concern to a BASE jumper, however, is the very object she is jumping off. BASE jumpers are more likely to be killed or injured colliding with the sides of a tower, or a jagged cliff face, than by hitting the ground at speed because their chute failed to fulfil its end of the bargain.

Contrary to popular belief, BASE jumping is not, in itself, illegal. However, accessing many sites, including such built landmarks as the Empire State Building, the Sydney Harbour Bridge or the Golden Gate Bridge in San Francisco, involves breaking trespassing laws. Ironically, the illicit nature of jumping from such sites both fuels the wrath of critics and lends anarchic appeal to the more reckless members of the BASE jumping community.

BEER-CAN boat racing

Racing boats made almost entirely from beer cans is an annual event in Darwin, Australia, a city where the only people bigger, tougher and thirstier than the local men are the local children. The feature event of a festival known as the Beer Can Regatta, the boat races take place in the warm waters off inner-city Mindil Beach; waters that have been known to accommodate large saltwater crocodiles, a fact that must play on the minds of crewmembers aboard vessels that are so thoroughly un-seaworthy they must surely have been built while the contents of the cans were being enthusiastically consumed.[1]

---

1 As a keenly fought consolation prize for boats that are as buoyant as a sack of river rocks, the regatta holds what is known as the Henley-on-Mindil. In this race, crewmembers have to carry and run with their boat across the sands of Mindil Beach.

The Beer Can Regatta has been held for more than 30 years. Its foundation is indelibly linked to Cyclone Tracy, which, on Christmas Eve 1974, tore through the tropical capital in Australia's far north, killing seventy-one people and devastating the city. It is the worst natural disaster in Australia's history. In the months following Cyclone Tracy, Darwin welcomed an influx of aid from interstate as the city looked to clean up and rebuild. Builders and various construction workers are thirsty at the best of times, but in Darwin's baking heat and shirt-drenching humidity they showed the town's beer supplies as little mercy as Tracy had shown Darwin.

The result of the increased beer drinking left aluminium beer cans lying around Darwin like spent bullet shells on a firing range. With no recycling programs in effect at the time, the cans were a considerable litter problem until one town resident, Lutz Frankenfeld, came up with the idea of holding a boat race, with all the boats having to be made entirely from 'empties', as drained beer cans are known. This, he felt, would give locals an incentive to go around town picking up all the discarded cans.

When the disbelief that anyone could actually be called Lutz Frankenfeld subsided, the plan was put into motion and in 1975 the inaugural Beer Can Regatta was held. Since then it has become a major event and a tourist attraction, with generated funds going to various charities. Like similar events around the world, it is also an excuse for organizers to liberally throw around puns and gags, as the event's so-called Ten Canmandments[2] illustrate.

----

2 According to the event's website (www.beercanregatta.org.au) the Regatta's Ten Canmandments are as follows:
  '1. Thou shalt enter the event in the right spirit.
  2. Thou shalt build the craft of cans.
  3. The craft shall float by cans alone.
  4. Thou shalt not drown.
  5. Thou shalt not take the name of the craft in vain. Any craft bearing signs or lettering that may be offensive will be barred.

The Beer Can Regatta also holds a host of water- and sand-based competitions (including a soft drink-can boat race for children), but the signature competition has always been the adult boat challenge, in which boats made 'substantially' from beer cans (there is an allowance for a wooden framework and binding materials) race each other within safe access of Mindil Beach. Complicating matters for boat builders is that each boat must carry a crew of four, which is four more than many of the boats are structurally capable of holding. Which, of course, is all part of the entertainment.

Other unashamedly silly races

WOK RACING

Devised in 2003 by a German television host with too much time on his hands, wok racing sees competitors using modified Chinese cooking woks as glorified toboggans to slide down an Olympic bobsleigh track (a winding open channel, 1.2–1.3 kilometres long, made of concrete and ice).

6. Thou shalt not drift from the straight and narrow and end up at Mandorah.
7. Thou shalt not protest too much.
8. Thou shall honour thy committee.
9. Thou shalt not commit adultery—nothing really to do with the Regatta, but it gives us an air of responsibility and respect.
10. Thou shalt go back and read the first canmandment again.'

Although wok racing is more an idle diversion than a serious sport, fully laden woks can reach speeds close to 90 kilometres per hour (for the individual competition) and 110 kilometres per hour (for the four-person competition, which sees each team-member seated within individual woks held together, one behind the other, by a frame). To allow them to reach such olive oil-burning speeds, the bottom of the wok they are sitting in is sometimes heated, though presumably not while they are in it. Friction is reduced further—just as the ridiculousness of the situation is intensified—by wok sledders taping big silver soup ladles to their feet so that the heels of their shoes do not rest on the ice and slow them down.

As with all ice sports, speed is of the essence, but striving for swiftness doesn't come without risk. For wok sledders, flipping their cooking conveyance on a tight corner is common, so they are kitted out in considerable protective gear. It's unlikely any have opted for additional cushioning by stuffing their leather suits with tofu, bok choy and oyster sauce, despite such a move proving rather convenient when the time comes for a celebratory dinner after competition.

Wok races were held in Winterberg, Germany, in 2003 and 2005 and in Innsbruck, Austria, in 2004, 2006 and 2007.

BATH TUB RACING

The harbour city of Nanaimo in British Columbia, Canada, likes to think of itself as the Bath Tub Racing Capital of the world; a title the rest of the world is

---

---

presumably happy to concede if it makes the Nanaimoans happy. The title comes from 40 years of hosting annual bathtub races; first from Nanaimo and Vancouver, and now in and around Nanaimo harbour with the finish line in Departure Bay.

Despite the name of the event, the bathtubs used in the race are highly modified. In short, conventional bathtub shells are fitted into a small racing hull, meaning the bathtub acts more as a cabin for the pilot to sit in than a flotation device. The tubs, however, must be old-style, rolled-edged baths with an outboard motor of no more than eight horsepower.

An arguably purer form of bathtub racing takes place every year on the River Meuse in Dinant, Belgium. Known as *La Régate Internationale des Baignoires* (the International Bathtub Regatta), the race began as a publicity stunt in the early 1980s to attract visitors to the small but picturesque town, which is about an hour from Brussels. During the race, townsfolk and tourists line the riverbanks as the flotilla of super-slow craft (done up like Mardi Gras floats) make their way along the river. Like Nanaimo's bathtub race, the competing craft in Dinant—a town known for its artisans—are modified bathtubs, but motors are not permitted, meaning paddle power is necessary.

Paddles and motors are useless in the annual bathtub race held in Nome, Alaska, primarily because it takes place on land—through the middle of town, to be precise. Old claw-foot-style baths are the most popular model and wheels are mounted on the legs. Each bath must have five crew members: four runners/pushers and one passenger who, in a nice touch, must be sitting

---

----

in a warm bubble bath. To prevent disqualification, every bath that crosses the finish line must contain a bar of soap, a towel, a bathmat and at least 10 gallons of water.

CARDBOARD BOAT RACING

For 30 years, Heber Springs in Arkansas, United States, has hosted cardboard boat races on Greers Ferry Lake. As cardboard and water are as naturally complementary as wind and broadsheet newspapers, most boats inevitably sink before they negotiate the 200-yard course, although a leaky boat may still win a prize for its design and appearance. The surprise, of course, is that any boats manage to stay afloat at all. Good craftsmanship is vital in this regard, as is the use of hard, corrugated cardboard for the boat's hull and the judicious use of duct tape, glue and resin. Before 1999, crew members were obliged to use hand paddles to power their craft, but now any human-powered propulsive device is permitted, such as foot-pedalled paddle wheels. Sensibly, life jackets are mandatory.

MILK CARTON DERBY

Like a healthy alternative to Darwin's Beer Can Regatta, Seattle's annual Milk Carton Derby is a race across Green Lake for boats made entirely from milk cartons. As with Arkansas' cardboard boat race, entrants put as much effort into appearance as they do into structural soundness, as separate prizes for such are on offer.

FURNITURE RACING

Every April since 1970, the US ski resort of Whitefish, Montana, has celebrated the end of ski season by sticking skis on various items of household furniture and finding passengers to race them down a snowy hill. That said, speed isn't the only criterion. The judges rightly take into account the majesty of a club lounge building up a head of steam as it careers down a snow-bound slope. Appearance and accuracy are also important and the furniture drivers must stop their craft (items of furniture entered into the competition must be fitted with a working brake) as close to a selected target as possible. Fittingly, there is no abiding definition of 'furniture' in use at Whitefish; couches, armchairs, coffee tables, toilets and even coffins have been raced.

Birling

Also known as logrolling, birling is a niche sport that grew out of the skills a North American lumberjack of old would use in transporting cut timber downriver to sawmills, a process known as river pigging.[1] Although logs are today driven to mills in the kind of enormous, bellowing trucks that sit on your tail and scare the bejesus out of you on lonely mountain roads, birling has survived as a sport and is almost exclusively contested at lumberjack competitions—which isn't to say anyone with their own swimming pool and a ready supply of logs couldn't host birling contests at home.

---

1 During the winter cutting season, in forests too deep for decent roads, orthodontists and rigorous personal hygiene, lumberjacks (now known as loggers) would transport logs to the banks of frozen rivers using ox and cart. In the spring thaw, river drivers would roll the logs into the water and drive the mass of timber downriver to strategically located sawmills. To manage this, the river drivers needed the dexterity of jungle cats as they stood atop the logs with only spiked boots and piked poles (poles with metal spikes on the end) to assist them. The mass of logs could number in the hundreds. Obviously it was dangerous work. One slip could see the river driver end up in the near-freezing

Birling is a competition between two fully clothed competitors[2] standing atop a log that is floating in a body of water. The object of the game is to be the last person standing on the log—something easier said than done once the competitors start rolling the log by walking or running on it in an attempt to dislodge the other competitor (skilled logrollers can also stop a rolling log, or even reverse its direction). At no time can a birler touch his opponent or make contact with the log with any part of his body other than his feet.[3]

Birling competitions typically begin with birlers stepping off a dock onto a floating log and steadying themselves with the help of attendants, who offer them wooden poles to hold on to. Once the birlers have pushed off from the dock, the referee asks them to steady the log and get their balance. When that

---

drink. If the cold wasn't enough to kill him, the clattering of the logs together could crush his head like a pimple. His most dangerous work was clearing log jams—the consequence of all those logs piling up at a kink in the river. Sometimes he'd have to resort to explosives, other times he could locate the one log that was the key to the jam and budge it. Having finally arrived at the sawmill, the river drivers would unwind with logrolling contests. In these, two or more men would stand on a floating log and 'roll it out' until only one remained high and dry.

2 The competitors are fully clothed for authenticity, not just because spectators would rather stick pins in their eyes than have to watch log rollers jiggle around on the water wearing next to nothing. Contrary to comedy troupe Monty Python's 'Lumberjack Song' (which referenced a high heel-, suspender- and bra-wearing lumberjack who wished he'd been a girlie), lumberjacks typically wore boots, trousers and heavy jackets, as they often transported logs along icy rivers in winter. None wore swimming costumes. And if any wore women's clothing, it was well hidden away.

3 According to the Lumberjack Water Sports' website (www.logrolling.org), prospective birlers should consider the following:

'Rule #1: No looking at your feet. Your feet are never going to leave the bottom of your legs, so there is no reason to look straight down at them …

… Contrary to popular belief, the real balance in logrolling is from the waist down, in your legs … A roller's knees must always be bent, as well as a

is done to his satisfaction he asks the birlers (much to the amusement of any spectators who relish a double entendre) to 'throw your poles'. From that point the contest is on until one competitor falls, or a time limit is reached. Should the latter occur, the contest resumes on a log with a smaller diameter—a smaller log being less stable in the water and thus more likely to lead to a result. In semi-finals and finals, logrolling contests are usually a best-of-five scenario.

Logs used for competition are commonly western red or western white cedar logs, stripped of bark and knots so that they are as smooth as possible. Consequently, competition birlers usually wear spiked shoes or boots to help with traction. In practice and amateur matches, however, many logs are carpeted (and presumably Scotchgarded to prevent water stains), which allows for easier traction. Such a practice has created controversy, especially now that many involved in the sport are calling for professional birling contests to be conducted on carpeted logs. Birling purists are horrified at the suggestion, seeing carpeted logs as an attack on the sport's integrity and traditions, not to mention a decorating disaster in the making.

---

roller's lower back. The lower you are, the lower center of gravity you have, and the harder it will be to get off balance …

Head and eyes should be focused on the other end of the log at all times. Remember Rule #1 of rolling? Never take your eyes off your opponent's feet. The same applies for practice. Your eyes should never leave the other end of the log.

Your feet must remain moving at all times … picking your feet up and down, just high enough for your spikes/shoes/feet to leave the log … pretend [you] are squashing ants. This helps get down the general rhythm. You may choose to move your feet faster or slower, depending on the variables at hand.'

Other logger sports

To celebrate the traditions and skills of those in the timber industry, various countries hold competitions for loggers. Though sometimes described as logger sports in North America, they are just as commonly referred to as lumberjack competitions (the so-called Lumberjack World Championships are held annually in Hayward, Wisconsin). In Australia and New Zealand, competitions for loggers centre around woodchopping and sawing, events well received at Australian agricultural shows. The events listed below may not necessarily be contested at all such competitions. Like logrolling, which is chiefly a North American concern, some are particular to a country and/or competition:

Underhand chop: The underhand chop has a woodchopper standing on a horizontally laid log with a 12-inch diameter. Using a 5-pound axe he cuts through it with downward blows. The first to sever his log is the winner.

Standing block: As above, except the log is vertical and the woodchopper stands astride it. Typically, he begins by cutting a scarf (a v-shaped cut) into one side until he reaches the centre. He then cuts a back scarf into the other side until the block is cut through.

Tree felling: With the block secured to the top of a tree or pole, the woodchopper scales the tree using three iron-tipped 'jigger boards', which he inserts into notches of varying height that are cut into the tree. Once he's ascended to the block, he attacks it with his axe, cutting halfway through it

----

before descending the tree, scaling the other side, again using the jigger boards and completing the severing of the block. A similar discipline is known in North America as the springboard chop.

Speed climbing (United States): Two 60-foot poles are placed side by side so that two competitors, wearing harnesses and specially designed shoes with spikes, can race each other to the top of the poles and back down again.

BoG Snorkelling

Seen through a poetic eye, peat bogs, like Keith Richards, have a kind of harsh, wind-scarred beauty and, unlike Keith Richards, are lovely places for a ramble. Alternatively, peat bogs are wet and cold with just the kind of desolation sought by those wishing to dispose of the odd corpse.[1] In short, not the sort of place you'd choose for a dip.

This goes no way to explain why, since 1986, the good people of Llanwrtyd Wells in central Wales have hosted the optimistically named World Bog Snorkelling Championships, or why people have actually turned up to compete. Were it not held at a different time of year, it would seem obvious

---

1 One ventures to guess that should you inadvertently interrupt a hit man disposing of a body on a bog, your poetic temperament will do you no good at all when he's vigorously chasing you down with a soil-spattered shovel. Best to throw yourself into the murky waters and frog stroke the hell out of there. If possible, take note of your time over 60 yards.

that Llanwrtyd Wells' hosting of an annual beer festival was more than mere coincidence.

Under championship rules, contestants are required to swim two lengths of a 60-yard trench cut into the Waen Rhydd peat bog.[2] Since peat bogs are essentially huge porous slabs of decomposing vegetation, the waters within are frigid, pungent, sludgy and murky at best, and about as conducive to swimming as cat food. Fortunately, in what one suspects is a nod to the UN's *Declaration of Human Rights*, competitors are allowed to wear fins and goggles (which increase competitors' visibility from nothing to the inch of blackness between their retinas and the inside of their goggles), while only the particularly stupid eschew the option of a wetsuit.

The rules further stipulate that competitors, who are allowed to use snorkels, must not use their arms to aid propulsion through the turgid water, which is home to frogs, tadpoles, newts and even black scorpions. This raises the possibility that someone thrashing around in distress may actually be disqualified before they are rescued.

Because bog water resembles a witch's brew, concerns for the health of competitors have often been raised, but local publican Gordon Green (the man credited with devising the event in order to turn around the fortunes of tiny Llanwrtyd Wells) has pointed out that bog water in the region is acidic enough to kill most bacteria; the thought-provoking word here being, of course, 'most'.

The World Bog Snorkelling Championships are held on the United Kingdom's August Bank Holiday and cost a small fee to enter. All moneys are donated to charity, which brings some sense to proceedings.

---

2 At the time of publication Welshman Philip John held the 'world record' of 1 minute 35 seconds.

Other bog sports

BOG CYCLING

Cycling a mountain bike through a watery trench cut into a peat bog makes
even less sense than swimming through one, but perhaps that was reason
enough for Llanwrtyd Wells to add the sport to its annual events calendar.

First contested in 1998, the World Mountain Bike Bog Snorkelling
Championships, held every July, requires competitors to cycle a mountain bike
two lengths of a 45-yard trench. The depth of the muddy trench (6 feet)
ensures that the bicycle (and most, if not all, of the cyclist) is fully submerged,
which makes the task more than difficult and, you could say, less than
sensible. As a small concession, the mountain bikes supplied by organizers
are weighted; their frames filled with lead and the tyres filled with water. This
counteracts the cyclist's buoyancy, keeping the wheels on the muddy bottom
of the bog and enabling 'normal' cycling to be achieved.

BOG TRIATHLON

If neither bog snorkelling nor bog cycling is appealing enough on its own, the
Bog Snorkelling Triathlon looks to fill the breach. Held the same July weekend
as the mountain bike event, the triathlon requires competitors to complete a
12-mile run, a 120-yard bog snorkel and a 19-mile mountain bike ride
through the Waen Rhydd Bog.

If the world was crying out for a sport that mixed volleyball, football (soccer), trampolining, the Brazilian martial art of capoeira *and* the hip-shaking vibe of samba, it was keeping its voice down. Nevertheless, in Spain during the last decade, Belgian music entrepreneur Filip Eyckmans rummaged around in his imagination and invented bossaball—not only a melange of the aforementioned ingredients but also, tellingly, a franchise for hire.

Perhaps the most distinctive feature of bossaball—one, ironically, that all but guarantees it will remain, like SlamBall (see page 35), a fringe sport—is the court itself. The size of a volleyball court, and with a volleyball net strung across it, it is entirely inflatable, like a child's jumping castle minus the walls, turrets and vomit. More distinctive still, on each side of the net in centre court, are two circular trampolines; each separated from the expanse of inflatable court by knee-height inflatable rings (bossawalls) about 1 metre wide. Considering such complexity, it will come as no surprise that it takes about 45 minutes to assemble the court, beyond the patience of the average child who, in any case, wouldn't have a backyard big enough to fit one in.

Bossaball is ideally a three, four or five-a-side game in which one player on each side remains stationed on his team's trampoline. As with volleyball, the object of the game is to propel the ball over the net so that it is grounded in the opponent's half of the court, or cannot be returned. One point is scored when this occurs, while three points are scored for grounding a ball on an opponent's trampoline. No points are scored—and the ball is considered to still be in play—when a ball strikes the bossawalls.

While volleyball allows three touches per team before the ball must be returned over the net (no one is allowed to touch it twice in a row), bossaball allows eight. This gives the trampoline-based player a number of chances to win a point with a dramatic spike (a powerful shot from above net height that is driven down rather than looped up and over) from metres in the air. Also different to volleyball is that bossaballers are allowed to keep the ball up and in play with any body part. Should they use their feet and head, as football (soccer) players are accustomed to, they are allowed two touches at any one time. For this reason, when played by all-round athletes, bossaball can be spectacular to watch, as acrobatic competitors know that in their quest to return a ball they can throw their bodies around with little risk of injury.

Being mostly an exhibition sport, bossaball doesn't necessarily require referees. The sport-cum-franchise is, however, keen to recruit referees to oversee impromptu competitions, which are usually set up at beaches, festivals, carnivals, shopping centres, schools and entertainment industry events. Interestingly, bossaball is seeking what it calls 'samba referees' who are not only equipped with a whistle but—somewhat tediously, sporting purists might think—a microphone, a number of percussion instruments and a disc jockey's deck.[1]

----

1 A referee-recruiting item in www.bossaball.com asks the following, rather
   chilling, questions. 'Do you like action sports? Are you a DJ? Do you have a funny

While bossaball has been launched in Belgium, the Netherlands, Spain and Brazil, it appears guaranteed to remain a sport mainly used as a marketing device—not least because members of the general public will rarely see it played and even more rarely play it themselves. As the sport's internet home page states:

> **Bossaball offers great opportunities for marketing and corporate branding. It attracts attention and often generates a large amount of media coverage including print, internet, radio and television, which makes bossaball an outstanding publicity support.**

This is not to suggest that many people don't enjoy playing or watching bossball, not least a significant number of poseurs—the tanned, lightly muscled type often found strutting around on Brazilian beaches in swimming costumes that don't leave enough to the imagination—who see it as another wonderful means of exhibiting themselves.

voice? Can we leave a game of bossaball to your judgment? Then you might have what it takes to become a samba referee!'

Another bouncy ball sport not taking the world by storm

SLAMBALL

Like bossaball, SlamBall is an entrepreneur's idea; in this case American Mason Gordon, who in the early 2000s strived to create a made-for-TV sport that replicated the supposed excitement of a video game.

Most similar to basketball, SlamBall, which looks like the kind of futuristic sport imagined in sci-fi films, is a four-on-four game played on a court similar in size to a basketball court with regulation baskets and backboards at each end. The most significant difference between the two courts—apart from the plexiglass surrounding the SlamBall court, as in ice hockey—is that SlamBall courts have four large trampolines situated around each basket, at ground level. These allow high-flying players to seemingly soar in the air and deliver gravity-defying slam dunks, which are worth three points (shots from the field are worth two). Another major difference to basketball is that SlamBall allows rigorous bodychecks. Due to this fact, and that players need to be protected from potentially rough landings, players wear skateboarding-style elbow, knee and wrist guards.

In 2002, the first Slamball season got underway in the United States. Team names more resembled gangs that might appear in a sequel to West Side Story: Bouncers, Diablos, Mob, Rumble, Slashers and Steal.

Outside of Canada, a broom tends to have one use, and that's to lean inside a cluttered cupboard in such a way that when the door is opened it topples out like a falling tree, as if to remind its owner how infrequently it is used for its intended purpose. In Canada, however, a broom has superseded its domestic roots to become a piece of sporting equipment in at least two games, broomball being one of them. Mops and dustpans everywhere must be green with envy.

Broomball is, for descriptive purposes, 'lite' ice hockey. Although players wear rubber-soled shoes instead of skates, broomball is played on an ice rink over 18-minute halves. The object of the six-a-side game is to score by propelling a ball (not a puck) into the opposition's goal. Instead of a hockey stick, however, broomball players use either a specialized 'broom', made with a triangular moulded-rubber head and aluminium shaft, or, traditionally, an actual broom, its bristles frozen or dipped in rubber to harden them. The ball can then be pushed between team-mates—or shunted about like a wad of dog hair across a kitchen floor—but most often it is thwacked, with the broomballer wielding her broom much like a hockey stick. The ball is about half the size of a football (soccer ball), and is made of hard, orange rubber. The goals, measuring 1.7 x 2.35 metres, are set in from each end, allowing players to move around them as in ice hockey.

With broomball players wearing shoes (the ice is kept dry to allow them to maintain grip), the game is significantly slower than ice hockey, in which players, obviously, wear skates. That said, it is still a fast-paced game and good players are adept not only at running over the ice but also at using the ice to their advantage in sliding to reach a ball that may have appeared just out of reach. Elite players are so good at this that even when skidding across the ice like penguins they can still pass the ball or shoot for goal.

Like ice hockey competitors, broomball players wear a good deal of protective equipment, such as helmets, face guards, shin pads, gloves, knee and elbow pads, and boxes; the latter being hard plastic cups that are placed in a strategic area so as to prevent male broomballers ever having to see wince-inducing footage of themselves on a *Funniest Home Videos*-style TV program. But since broomball is ostensibly a non-contact sport, the equipment serves to protect players from errant broom swings and falls on the concrete-hard ice. Some leagues, however, allow a player to 'check', or shoulder charge, an opponent if that opponent has the puck or has just passed it. Checking from behind, like tripping, elbowing and lifting the stick above shoulder height, will incur penalties.

It is said that broomball was first played in Canada in the early 1900s, using frozen ponds as rinks and standard brooms as sticks. It's believed to have been particularly popular with tram workers in Montreal, who played it with a small football (soccer ball) and the corn brooms they used to sweep snow and mud from the tram rails. Popular as a social game in Canada, it soon spread to the northern US states, but it wasn't until the 1960s that competitive leagues began to pop up, along with a move to playing the game indoors with a now specialized broom and ball.

Broomball leagues of varying sizes are now found in more than a dozen countries, including Canada, the United States, Italy, Germany, Sweden, Japan and Australia. The International Federation of Broomball Associations is run out of Canada and oversees the bi-annual World Broomball Championships which, to date, have been dominated by Canada.

Some other ice sports

CURLING

Perhaps the best-known broom-and-ice sport is curling, not least because it is a Winter Olympic sport[1], one widely played in Canada and Scotland. Resembling lawn bowls, shuffleboard and bocce, curling is a precision sport in which players look to slide a granite stone shaped like a cheese wheel down a 44.5 metre runway of ice (known as a 'sheet') towards a bulls-eye target (known as a 'house') painted on the ice. Points are scored for the

---

---

1 Curling was on the Winter Olympics program in 1924, but disappeared soon afterwards. It was a demonstration sport in 1932, 1988 and 1992, before again being officially included in 1998. Since then, separate tournaments for men and women have been held.

number of stones a four-member team 'delivers' (pushes) closest to the centre of the house (a circle with a 30 centimetre diameter known as the 'button'), relative to an opponent's closest stones.[2]

One of the most distinctive features of curling is the very thing that often makes non-curling nations smirk, and that's all the broom sweeping that goes on—frequently with the vigour of a couple of teenagers looking to clean up the house after a wild party the night before, knowing their parents will be home any second.

Brooms, the heads of which are now more like brushes, come into curling once a stone has been delivered by one team-member sliding gracefully, almost tenderly, onto one knee as she pushes the 19.1 kilogram stone away from her using a small handle on the stone's upper side. With the stone (which is gently rounded on the bottom and the top) in motion, two team-mates, each with a broom in hand, precede it down the sheet in case their team captain, the skip, believes its momentum or direction needs changing (curling sheets are sprayed with water before play, creating a slight pebbling effect which, due to friction, causes the stone to curve, particularly as it gets closer to the house). If the skip believes that's the case, she yells instructions

2 For example, if the closest stone to the button is from Team A, and the second closest is from Team B, then Team A scores one point and Team B scores nothing. If the closest and second closest stones are from Team A, Team A scores two points, and so on. This means that for each of the game's eight to ten rounds (called ends), points per round are never split. One team will always score zero.

to the sweepers, who sweep the section of ice in front of the moving stone. Their action momentarily melts the ice, thereby lessening friction and allowing the stone to travel a fraction further than it would have done without such intervention. Such sweeping can also change the degree of curve on a stone—usually reducing it.

The name curling does not, as it would seem, come from the motion of the stone once it has been delivered. It derives from the verb *curr*, from the Scots language, which describes a low rumble— just the kind of noise a curling stone makes as it travels over the pebbled ice. In Scotland, where records indicate curling was around as early as the 1500s, the game is still known as 'the roarin' game'. There, as in Canada, it is much loved,[3] although it is played

3 **'Curlers' Grace'**
   O'Lord wha's love surrounds us a',
   And brings us a' the gether,
   Wha' writes your laws upon oor hearts,
   And bids us help each ither.
   We bless Thee for Thy bounties great,
   For meat and hame and gear,
   We thank Thee, Lord, for snaw and ice,
   But still we ask for mair.
   Gi'e us a hert to dae whit's richt,
   Like curlers true and keen,
   To be guid friends along life's road,
   And soop oor slide aye clean.
   O Power abune [above] whose bounty free,

in numerous other countries, to varying degrees, including the United States, Japan, Sweden, Norway, Denmark, Finland and Australia.

Whether it's accurate to say curling is sweeping the world off its feet is another matter.

BANDY

Although players use ice hockey equipment, including skates and a hockey stick, bandy is essentially field hockey played on ice. Accordingly, bandy players—who use a hard rubber ball instead of a puck—have fewer missing teeth than their ice hockey counterparts. Played mostly in northern Europe, bandy is an eleven-a-side game of 45-minute halves played on a football pitch-sized area (in this case covered in ice), where the goals (2.1 metres by 3.5 metres) are located midway along each end line.

As with field hockey, teams look to score by hitting the ball with their sticks into the opposition's goal. Again, like field hockey, players tend to make

Oor needs and wants suffices,
We render thanks for Barley Bree [whisky],
And meat that appetises.
Be Thou our Skip throughout life's game,
An' syne [since] we're sure to win,
Tho' slow the shot and wide the aim,
We'll soop [sweep] each ither in.
    —A prayer, of sorts, from the Royal Caledonian Curling Club in Edinburgh, Scotland, formed in 1843 and believed to be the world's oldest curling club.

---

formations linking defenders, midfielders and forwards, and there are no restrictions on who can go where on the field. Goalkeepers are the only players allowed to handle the ball; however, they can only do so within their own penalty area.

Because a ball is used in place of a puck, it's not uncommon for players to loft the ball with their sticks, as happens in field hockey. This leads to often spectacular scoring strokes that bring to mind a tennis player hitting a winner—although a bandy player will be penalized for lifting her stick above shoulder height. Unlike ice hockey sticks, the blades of bandy sticks may be wrapped with leather straps to help put spin on the ball.

Bandy, of course, is just one of many ball-and-stick games (like Irish hurling and Scottish shinty, for instance) which can be said to trace its roots back to ancient civilizations in Greece, Egypt and Iran. However, the game's modern roots appear to have taken hold at Bury Fen, northeast England, in the middle of the eighteenth century. The official rules of bandy were compiled in 1891 with the formation of the National Bandy Association of England.

The Federation of International Bandy was formed in 1955 and occasional world championships were held until 2003. Since then, annual championships have taken place. Russia (and the former Soviet Union) and Sweden have dominated both the men's and women's championships.

RINGETTE

A sport devised in Canada in 1963, primarily for girls and women, ringette is similar to ice hockey, except players use straight sticks in order to pass, carry and shoot a rubber ring measuring 16.5 centimetres in diameter. Teams of six (one of whom is a goalkeeper) score by shooting the ring into their opponents' goal. A number of rules exist to prevent a single player carrying the ring from end to end, thus making the game more inclusive to all players on the rink. One such rule demands competitors pass or shoot a ring within 5 seconds of receiving it. The World Ringette Championships are held annually.

RINK BANDY (RINKBALL)

Popular in Finland, particularly at school level, rink bandy is a diminutive form of bandy; it is played on an ice-hockey rink with only five players per side.

As part of the Fiesta de San Fermin, the ancient Basque city of Pamplona in northern Spain hosts the famed 'running of the bulls', or *encierro*, every 7–14 July. People flock to Pamplona from around the world for the chance to be gored, trampled or flung into the air by one or more rampaging 500-plus kilogram bulls.[1] Since 1910, at least fifteen people have succeeded in getting themselves killed while undertaking this endeavour; one romanticized many times in literature.[2] One of the most tragic runs took place in 1947 when the same bull, 'Semillero', killed two people. His feats were matched in 1980 by a bull named 'Antioquio'.

---

1 Of course many people flock to Pamplona simply to watch someone get gored, trampled or flung into the air by one or more rampaging 500-plus kilogram bulls.

2 American writer and man's man Ernest Hemingway wrote about the bull run in his 1926 novel *The Sun Also Rises*. In that book, and in his 1932 memoir

The purpose of the bull run is to transfer to the bullring the six bulls that will be used in the day's bullfighting (see page 46). To the outsider, it's not clear why the bulls aren't simply driven over in a truck. It would be less spectacular, certainly, and the chances of its making news bulletins around the world would be slim, but it would cut down on injuries, fatalities and the general mayhem caused by crowds of runners wearing traditional red scarves frantically trying to outpace a snorting, muscular knot of distressed bovines.

Be that as it may, bull runners are, unlike the bulls, an unusual breed, for the point is not to run miles ahead of the bulls as they charge down a narrow, cobbled, fenced-off route from the Santo Domingo enclosure[3] to the Plaza de Toros, but to stay tantalizingly close to the pointy end of the charging herd. Inevitably, close often becomes too close.

There are no formal guidelines issued by local officials as to what runners should do when the herd catches them up, but it's generally accepted that screaming out in abject horror before falling awkwardly onto your face as a bull stomps on your back is a good place to start. Alternatively, if you do not have your grandmother on hand to push her into the bull's path in order to save yourself, you can throw yourself into the air like a rag doll as a 12-inch horn pierces, if you're lucky, your buttocks.

The distance between Santo Domingo and the Plaza de Toros is about 825 metres and after the bulls are released at precisely 8 am (a rocket is fired to announce the moment), it generally takes the animals four minutes to

----

Death in the Afternoon, he all but glorified bullfighting, seeing it as a kind of choreographed ballet between artist (the matador) and beast.

3 Many runners, when waiting for the release of the bulls outside Santo Domingo, sing a traditional song to distract themselves from the dilating of their sphincters. The song translates as, 'We ask San Fermin, as our Patron, to guide us through the bull run and give us his blessing'.

complete the run, not counting the extra time that may be required to adequately trample runners in their path. When all the bulls are safely in their pens another rocket is fired in the air.

For those who come off second best during the running of the bulls, revenge comes in the afternoon when all six bulls are slowly killed in the bullring.

A parody of the bull run takes place on July 15 when revellers run in front of the early morning bus that comes past Santo Domingo. It's unclear if anyone has been injured or killed while doing this.

Other bovine sports

BULLFIGHTING

A controversial tradition in Spain, the bullfight (*corrida*) is a highly ritualized and deliberately stylistic event, during which a matador and his entourage step into an enclosure with a large bull (of the unlucky *toro bravo* breed, which are raised specifically for the sport) with the ultimate aim of killing it. While this is done as artistically as possible, it is unlikely the bull finds this any kind of consolation when it's in its death throes.

At the beginning of each fight (there are usually six on a program) the matador's assistants, three *banderilleros* (flagmen), taunt the bull by inviting it to attack their capes. The purpose of this is to allow the matador an

----

opportunity to assess the bull's behaviour, such as which horn it favours when attacking, and which direction it favours when it has to turn. Following the *banderilleros*, the matador confronts the bull, attempting to get as close as possible to the charging animal while at the same time remaining composed and graceful in his movements.

After the matador's first confrontation with the bull, two *picadors* (lancers) enter the bullring on heavily padded but blindfolded horses. Encouraging the bull to attack the horses (presumably the blindfolds are used so the horses can't see this egregious betrayal), the *picadores* stab the bull's neck with lances in order both to lower the bull's blood pressure (to prevent it having a heart attack, thus dying too early and spoiling the fun) and to temper its strength (thereby finetuning the bull's charging tendencies based on what the matador has observed so far), so that the matador can take on greater risk. This is actually seen as a test of the bull's bravery and an insight into how much fight he has in him. A bull with little fight is a disgrace to the breeder, although, again, it's unlikely the bull has his breeder's honour in mind when the *picadores* are drawing his blood.

Following the *picadores*, the *banderilleros* return to the ring. Each of them attempts to plant two *banderillas* (barbed sticks decorated with little flags) into the bull's neck. This further weakens the bull and, if done correctly, makes him drop his head and horns, allowing the matador more latitude.

Finally the matador returns to the action with a *muleta* (a small red cape) in one hand and, not boding well for the bull, a sword in the other. During this section of the fight, called the *faena* (work), the matador does his best to impress the crowd by encouraging the bull into a series of close passes. Contrary to popular belief, bulls are not enraged by the colour red. They are, in fact, colour blind, and are simply attracted by the motion of the cape. At the conclusion of his cape work the matador manoeuvres the bull into a position where he can kill it by driving his sword through its shoulder blades and into its heart. Although hardly enough to gain credit from animal welfare groups, failure to kill the bull quickly can significantly undermine a matador's performance.

Bullfighting is also practised in Portugal and parts of Latin America but, as in Spain, it's a tradition under threat from animal welfare groups.

COW FIGHTING

A traditional event popular in the Swiss canton of Valais, cow fighting is the result of human beings facilitating a naturally occurring phenomenon whereby cows of a certain breed wrestle among themselves to determine the head of the herd. Stereotyping suggests that the Swiss aren't known for their sense of humour, and although cow fighting doesn't exactly overturn this perception (arguably it's more bizarre than funny), it does at least suggest they are trying.

Placed together in a ring, with any sharp horns blunted, the cows—all from the local Vache d'Hérens breed—are encouraged to sort themselves into a pecking order. As mentioned, this is something the small-bodied, black and brown cows do naturally every spring when the change in the air carries with it delusions of grandeur. Due to their relative lack of aggression (compared to

----

bulls, that is), fighting cows tend to lock horns and engage in a push-and-shove contest. Any cow that chickens out from a fight is shooed away by adjudicators armed with sticks until only one cow, *la reine* (the queen), remains. At the end of the season, in May, a grand final is held in Aproz, where the best cows from each district do battle in six weight categories. At the end of it all, *la reine des reines* (the queen of queens) is crowned.

For those whose entertainment requirements have nothing to do with cows (steaks and hamburgers notwithstanding), it may seem difficult to believe that cow fights attract spectators. But as many as 40,000 people have attended the dozen cow fighting events held every year in Valais.

Buzkashi

Afghanistan is not a good place to be a goat if the Afghan national sport of *buzkashi* is any indication. Translated as 'goat grabbing', the traditional sport sounds at first like something lonely men in remote regions might indulge in to pass the interminable hours. However, *buzkashi* is more like rugby on horseback, with the carcass of a goat (or calf) used as a ball, or *boz*[1]. Either way, it is not something upon which animal protection organizations would look favourably.

Buzkashi, a popular team game in Central Asia, was banned during the recent rule of the Taliban in Afghanistan. It is believed that the sport dates back to the days of Genghis Khan, when the Mongols played it on the steppes—the semi-arid grasslands shared by the likes of Afghanistan, Kazakhstan,

---

1 The goat or calf used in buzkashi is prepared for play by being beheaded, disembowelled, and denuded of limbs below the knee. It is then soaked in cold water for a day to toughen it. Sometimes, to give it more weight, the *boz* is filled with sand. Unlike balls used in most other sports, a *boz* is not the sort of thing Afghan children are likely to beg their parents for as a birthday present.

Uzbekistan, Russia and Turkmenistan. The nomads of the region, it is said, were highly skilful horsemen who could lean over and grab an animal from the ground while riding at full gallop, which must have been handy if they were running late for dinner.

Buzkashi requires just such skill and more. It has few rules of conduct (curiously, tripping a horse is forbidden, whipping a fellow competitor is not), but requires considerable toughness, endurance and strength. Not only does the carcass weigh about 55 kilograms, but also the action gets rough within the snorting, dust-strewn scrum of man and beast.[2] Broken limbs and even death have resulted from bad falls, while more superficial injuries are common, with whips and flying boots often used to keep competitors at bay. Considering some games can last all day, one presumes a rider's rank body odour may also serve as a disincentive to opponents looking to get close and personal.

There are two variations of *buzkashi*. The simplest version, *tudabarai*, requires the rider who has managed to grab hold of the carcass to ride in any direction until clear of the game's other players. Considering a hundred riders may be taking part, this is easier said than done. Quite often a rider carrying the *boz* may be on the verge of breaking free of the pack, victory in his sights, when the *boz* is suddenly yanked from his possession.

In the other version of the game, *qarajai*, a rider who has managed to get hold of the *boz* attempts to carry it around a marker about 1 kilometre away, before

----

2 The horses used in buzkashi are highly trained. As well as being quick and powerful, they know to stop in their tracks when their rider is thrown. Horses used in buzkashi are often not owned by the riders, but by wealthy men who can afford to hire trainers. The owner of the horse rewards the winning rider (commonly with money or gifts, such as fine clothes), for a win brings the horse considerable fame.

tossing it into his team's scoring circle. In each version of *buzkashi*, points are awarded for getting control of the *boz* and getting it into the scoring area.

Scoring, however, is not something most players get to enjoy. Only the most skilful riders (called *chapandaz*) even get close to the *boz*, let alone carry it for a score. Considering what the *boz* actually is, one might think that that's not always such a bad thing.

Other bestial sports

TUNA TOSSING

Port Lincoln, South Australia, is home to Australia's tuna fishing fleet. Since the fleet also holds licences to catch bluefin tuna for the lucrative Japanese market, Port Lincoln is said to have more millionaires per capita than any other town in Australia. In celebration of this fact the town hosts an annual festival called 'Tunarama', the highlight of which—depending on your definition of highlight, of course—is a tuna tossing competition. Who says Australia lacks culture?

The competition (held every year over the Australia Day long weekend in late January) sees entrants attempting to throw a frozen 8–10 kilogram tuna as far as possible without overstepping the mark. As such, it resembles the hammer

---

throw. Not surprisingly, the current record holder, with a 37.23-metre throw, is a former Olympic hammer thrower, Australian Sean Carlin.

In respect to the tuna used, good sense prevails, as the fish has already been deemed unsuitable for the dinner table.

MULLET TOSSING

Taking place every April on a beach on the border of Florida and Alabama, the Interstate Mullet Toss works on similar principles to the tuna toss, except the mullets used are not frozen. Indeed, it is permissible when tossing a mullet from Alabama into Florida to screw the 1-pound mullet up into a ball shape, if you think it'll be more aerodynamic that way. To be in with a chance of throwing the mullet the farthest, you'd need a toss of about 100 feet. Unfortunately, being a hardy fish, the mullet tends to unfold in the air, making flight less efficient. At the end of the event, mullets used in the toss are fed to the birds.

CRICKET SPITTING

As the name suggests, cricket spitting is a sport where contestants place a dead cricket in their mouth and then spit it out as far as possible. The sport, if you can call it that, was devised in 1997 by entomologist Tom Turpin at Purdue University in Indiana, United States. The competition is held during the university's annual Bug Bowl, a kind of entomological festival. Pennsylvania State University also holds an annual cricket spit.

Rules vary between competitions but generally the crickets are Brown House crickets (weighing between 45 and 55 milligrams) that have been previously frozen and then thawed. The contestant must be standing within the spitting circle, and the cricket must be fully intact when it lands, for a spit to be measured.

GOOSE GRABBING

Now banned, for reasons that will become glaringly obvious, goose grabbing was played in the seventeenth century when New York was a Dutch colony. A challenge to both a competitor's hand–eye co-ordination and stomach for violence, goose grabbing involved smearing the neck of a live goose with oil or soap then hanging it upside down between two poles. Competitors on horseback would then ride towards it at full gallop and, in passing, attempt to rip its head off. Unfortunately for the goose this was not always achieved at the first attempt.

PATO

Another controversial game, first played by *gauchos* (Argentine cowboys) in the seventeenth century, *pato* was a very similar sport to buzkashi, since a competitor's objective was simply to attain possession of a 'ball' amid a scrum of fellow competitors and ride with it to the outskirts of the field (which could have been the distance between neighbouring ranches). In the case of *pato*, the ball was a (temporarily) live duck, the body of which, for reasons that could never make sense, was encased in a leather pouch with handles. It's not difficult to imagine the trepidation that must have come over an Argentine duck in the seventeenth century when it found itself captured and being measured up for a tiny leather outfit. 'I've got a baaaad feeling about this,' it might have thought. 'Are those handles? Tell me those aren't handles.'

In the 1930s, after a long period in which the game was effectively banned on account of its cruelty and dangerous nature, *pato* (which is Spanish for 'duck') was resurrected and regulated. Instead of a duck as its centrepiece, the sport used a ball with six leather handles. Furthermore, a more conventional scoring system was implemented—a system still in place under the Federación Argentina de Pato (loosely, and wonderfully, translated as the Argentine Federation of Duck). In *pato*, competing riders, on two teams of four players, attempt to throw the ball through vertical hoops (1 metre in diameter) that are atop 2.4-metre poles at opposite ends of a ground resembling a polo field. Having gained possession of the *pato* a rider must hold it at the end of his outstretched arm, as if offering it to his competitors. If a competitor attempts to tug the *pato* away, both riders must stand on their stirrups for the duration of the tug, or *cinchada*.

The game lasts for six 7-minute periods, although play continues after the 7-minute mark if a tug is in process, ending when the *pato* falls to the ground.

The resurrection of *pato* was complete when, in 1953, the Argentine Congress declared it Argentina's national sport.

Not exactly a sport to take the kids to see if you don't want them waking up screaming in the middle of the night, cage fighting is a popular description for a sometimes brutal combat sport more correctly known as mixed martial arts.

With links to both the ancient Greek sport of pankration (a boxing–wrestling hybrid) and the 1920s Brazilian fighting form known as *vale tudo* ('anything goes' in Portuguese), mixed martial arts sees athletes from different fighting disciplines matching wits and, to make it even more compelling, fists, feet, knees, forearms and elbows. It's like boxing, wrestling, judo, karate, jujitsu and tae kwon do rolled into one.

As the colloquial name of the sport implies, such match-ups—which are contested over three 5-minute rounds—commonly occur within a chain-link cage, around which often clamours the kind of fan one might suspect is more likely to spend his recreational hours throwing rocks at cats than, say, reading Dickens.[1] While the octagonal cage creates a distinctive marketing device, some, even within the sport, have suggested that it projects a poor image and perpetuates the belief of critics that the sport is barbaric. Others suggest the violence within the ring does a good enough job of that on its own, particularly in non-sanctioned competitions, which are sometimes held in the car parks of bars and, consequently, more resemble street fights.

Given the varied skills of combat athletes, cage fighting is, on paper at least, an interesting idea.[2] In reality, however, why someone would volunteer to step into a cage with the human equivalent of a wolverine is, along with the success of Keanu Reeves, one of life's many mysteries. Clearly, there can be no doubting the *courage* of cage fighters; their *sanity*, however, is another thing entirely.

Cage fighting had its genesis in the United States in 1993, when an organization called Ultimate Fighting Championship (UFC) began hosting cable-TV broadcast tournaments where bouts took place inside an octagonal cage. When it first started, the UFC promoted what was termed 'no holds barred' fighting because almost anything was allowed, aside from eye-gouging and striking the groin of an opponent. This meant that should a fighter— wearing fingerless gloves that have a minimum of padding—wish to kneel on the chest of an opponent and repeatedly bring the point of his elbow down on

---

1 Of course, it should be noted that penchants for tormenting cats and reading Dickens are not necessarily mutually exclusive. It's just that many cage-fighting fans don't so much cheer as bay.

2 Interesting, yes, but it could be argued that the purity of the original concept has been quickly watered down now that competitors have learned it's in their best interests to adopt skills from the other fighting disciplines. Arguably, grappling skills are even more important than striking skills.

the bridge of his opponent's nose, well, no one was going to stop him. This also meant that no-holds-barred fighting was banned by dozens of US states, with one senator likening it to 'human cock fighting'.

Since then, in an attempt both to protect fighters and to widen the appeal of the sport, more rules have been put into place by some of the larger organizing bodies such as the UFC and the PRIDE Fighting Championships, which is run out of Japan. While rules vary between organizations, they generally forbid a number of techniques in addition to those already mentioned. That is, no eye-gouging, biting, small joint manipulation or fish hooking.[3] This still allows a lot of room for creativity. Not all events, for instance, ban head-butts, elbow strikes, spinal locks and kneeing an opponent's head when he is on the ground. Nor do they ban visual offences, such as tacky tattoos, which are inordinately popular among cage fighters.

As with most fighting sports, victory in cage fighting is decided by the judges' decision, referee's stoppage, knockout, a competitor's corner man throwing in the towel and, most sensibly, submission—as in 'For the love of God stop hitting me, I give up!'

----

3 Fish hooking is sticking your finger into someone's mouth, curling it onto the inside of the cheek and pulling hard.

Some less painful martial arts

CAPOEIRA

A Brazilian martial art set to music, *capoeira* (pronounced cap-wear-a) resembles dancing as much as fighting. With participants forming a circle, or *roda*, two take it in turns to step forward into the centre and spar while the others play instruments and sing, responding to, or setting the tempo of, the bout. With no intention of actually making contact with each other, the two nominal combatants perform a series of sweeping and often breathtakingly acrobatic moves—as slow or as fast as each *capoeirista* can handle. High kicks, spinning kicks, handstands and feints are all common moves. Skilled *capoeira* opponents appear to be working in tandem—like dancers, or interlocking cogs—rather than against each other.

The origin of *capoeira* is in dispute, but one theory posits that African slaves, shipped by the Portuguese to South America (mainly Brazil) in the sixteenth century, created this martial art. Far from home and oppressed by their captors, the slaves practised *capoeira* as both a pleasurable pursuit and a disguised form of self-defence that was continued after slavery was abolished three hundred years later. At that time, however, it was viewed as an anti-authoritarian activity (perhaps because it was often practised by gangs of now emancipated, and unemployed, slaves). In Brazil, in the late 1800s, anyone caught practising *capoeira* was severely punished, some by having their Achilles tendons severed.

Today *capoeira* is an above-board activity that proponents say is practised on every continent, barring Antarctica where, presumably, it is too cold to contemplate stripping down to just a pair of light cotton trousers and 'moving to the rhythm'.

T'AI CHI CH'UAN

Like kung fu on Valium, *t'ai chi ch'uan*, or just *t'ai chi*, is a non-contact martial art in which exponents practise various moves and routines in elegant slow motion. Accordingly, should you ever get into a slow-motion fight, it would be wise to steer clear of a *t'ai chi* master, who could unhurriedly take you to pieces. That said, *t'ai chi* is mainly practised today as a physical and spiritual therapy, similar in its goals to yoga. Practised with un-flexed muscles and a gentleness of expression, *t'ai chi* is seen by some as a moving meditation that just happens to be good for the circulatory system. This makes it popular among older folk who, in China, Hong Kong and many cities around the world, can be seen performing *t'ai chi* in parks early in the morning, like so many trees swaying gently in the breeze.

CANE TOAD racing

Cane toad racing is a quirky pub entertainment mostly found in far north Queensland, Australia. Established for the purposes of amusing lubricated European backpackers, light-hearted charity collection, and pest eradication (though not necessarily in that order), a cane toad race tends to take place within a pub's beer garden, with a male or female pub employee—often identified by a laconic set to their mouth—overseeing events. This includes taking entry fees or donations from punters, who can only select a toad on gut instinct since any notion of 'form', in racing terms, is illusory.

A cane toad race is under starter's orders when a bucket containing six or so toads is placed upside down in the centre of a large circle drawn on the ground. The race begins when the starter lifts the bucket, allowing the toads, differentiated by ribbons or markers, to make their way in any direction towards the finish line. Of course, since it's highly unlikely the toads know, let alone care, they are in a race, many may choose to simply stay put and daydream about their reign of terror over Australia's tropical north.[1]

Sooner or later, however, some intrepid toad breaches the finish line. And when it does, it is supposedly customary in some pubs for the backer of the winning toad to give it a kiss. Considering cane toads are toxic, have a bloated, leprous look about them, and can reach the size of guinea pigs, this can somewhat offset the pleasure of winning.

If the toads themselves experience any pleasure in competition it is soon put to an end as, at the end of the day's racing, the losing cane toads are killed— along with the winning cane toad. In this, the culling of competitors, cane toad racing differs from almost every other form of animal racing except, perhaps, cockroach racing which, coincidentally or not, is another pub-based entertainment in Queensland (see opposite).

While antipathy towards cane toads is high in Queensland (an unofficial pastime among young and/or intellectually young residents is to kill cane toads by whacking them with golf clubs or cricket bats, or running them down in a car), wildlife officials urge that cane toads be disposed of humanely; something best achieved by placing the toads in a plastic bag and then into a freezer. It's believed the cold puts the toads to sleep before they quietly move on to the great sugar cane field in the sky.

----

1 In 1935, in an attempt to combat beetles that were destroying sugar cane crops, about 100 cane toads (*Bufo marinus*) were exported from Hawaii to Gordonvale in northern Queensland. Big mistake. Not only did the toads fail to keep insect numbers down, they quickly established themselves as a far worse pest and an environmental disaster. Cane toads, which are native to South America, are large enough to eat small native animals, while larger predators, and household pets, can be poisoned by eating or even mouthing the noxious amphibians. To date, there is no known method to control the all-but-indestructible cane toad and, as a result, the toads are slowly encroaching across the tropical north towards Western Australia and south towards New South Wales at a rate of 1.3 kilometres a year.

Other animals raced with or without human jockeys (and with or without sanction from animal protection groups) include:

BUFFALOES

During an annual water buffalo festival in Chonburi, Thailand, jockeys race buffaloes bareback on a 130-metre track.

CAMELS

This is a jockey sport popular in the Middle East, particularly the United Arab Emirates. There is also a camel race, The Camel Cup, held annually in Alice Springs, Australia.

COCKROACHES

Cockroach racing takes place in many countries around the world. Since 1982, when the inaugural winner was a roach named Soft Cocky, the Story Bridge Hotel in Brisbane, Queensland, has held the Australia Day Cockroach Races. Participants can bring their own cockroach or purchase one from the bar.

CRABS

Crab racing is similar to cane toad and cockroach racing but with crabs.

DOGS

Greyhound and whippet races are held worldwide. And once a year, in San Diego, California, dachshunds are raced in the so-called Wiener Nationals. In Canada, dog sled racing (where a team of dogs pull a sled on which a driver stands), over varying distances, is a popular winter sport (see page 105).

ELEPHANTS

During certain festivals, elephant races take place in parts of India, Nepal and Thailand.

HORSES

An age-old sport popular around the world, horses are raced in every conceivable way; over short distance, long distance, cross country, jumps and, in trotting and pacing, with rider-bearing buggies or sulkies attached.

LIZARDS

Eulo, Queensland, is home to the annual world lizard racing championships.

PIGEONS

The thoroughbred pigeon is said to be the fastest racing animal in the world. Pigeon racing—over varying distances—is popular in many countries. Normally, competing pigeons are removed a predetermined distance from their respective home coops and released at a specified time.

PIGS

Popular at fairs in the southern United States, pigs, usually juveniles, race around a circular track for entertainment rather than for betting purposes.

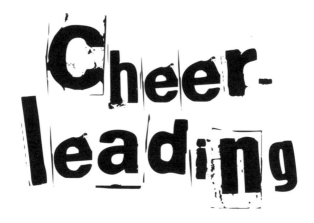

Cheer-leading

Until the 1970s, cheerleading was a relatively innocent activity whereby young girls, and sometimes very brave young men,[1] performed often highly athletic dance routines and tried to evoke partisan crowd support at American football matches, played by their respective high school or college teams. Although short skirts were a normal part of the uniform, and cheerleaders were often praised and admired by the student body (particularly the males—and certainly not because they had an admiration for formation dancing), there remained an apple pie-wholesomeness about the chirpy activity, which began to be considered a sport in its own right when cheerleading competitions started in the 1960s.

----

1 Male cheerleaders are often boorishly suspected of being fans of, well, let's just say, pianist Liberace's oeuvre—not that there's anything wrong with that. It could be countered, however, that male cheerleaders spend considerably more time in the company of female cheerleaders than their male counterparts on the football team, who, as it happens, shower together after training and matches.

To the horror of those who, with some justification, find chirpiness and wholesomeness (manufactured or not) stomach churning, cheerleading of this nature still takes place today. And while the chants, called cheers, are uncompromisingly daft, the physically demanding routines have become more complex and athletic, sometimes incorporating the kind of acrobatics performed by gymnasts and circus tumblers. Despite this, many people's understanding of cheerleading has been thrown into disarray, and even disapproval, by another strata of cheerleaders who spend as much time shaking their pom-poms as they do shaking their, well, pom-poms, if you get the gist.

This style of cheerleading—which borrows much from the shared fantasies of adolescent boys and balding middle managers with fat fingers—began in the United States' professional National Football League in the 1970s, with the pacesetters being the Dallas Cowboys Cheerleaders. Relying less on acrobatics and more on high kicks and star jumps performed in tiny white shorts and hopelessly outgunned crop tops, the Dallas Cowboys Cheerleaders became an iconic example of the advertising maxim 'sex sells'. For a certain breed of fan[2] such cheerleaders became as much a reason to attend a football match as the football match itself.

While both varieties of cheerleading are common in the United States today, it's principally the second variety that was exported to the rest of the world, such as the United Kingdom and Australia. Both the latter's National Rugby League and National Basketball Association, for example, tend to have as cheerleaders women in their late teens and early twenties who don't mind cavorting around in outfits that wouldn't look out of place in a red-light district. Their tight threads and largely decorative duties have critics labelling this form

2 … a certain breed some might describe as 'sad, desperate little men'; or at least men who don't get out nearly enough.

of cheerleading anachronistic and sexist. When they perform—such as at half-time, or after their team registers points on the scoreboard—the routines are not generally the type that would earn their choreographers awards or inspire note-taking from watching gymnasts.

Though often lampooned,[3] traditional cheerleading is, by contrast, taken very seriously by many US high schools and colleges. Moreover, cheerleading competitions are attracting made-up teams (who may have up to thirty-five members) not affiliated with any school or college. Such teams are often referred to as 'all-stars'. Today there are many competitions open to cheerleading teams (both school-based and all-stars) at local, state, national and even international level. In such competitions (which separate teams into various divisions depending on the age of the performers and the degree of difficulty of their routine), routines generally last $2^1/2$ minutes and attempt to marry dance, acrobatic stunts (such as tumbling, flips and human pyramids) and, if applicable, cheers.

The annual United States All Star Federation for Cheer and Dance Teams (USASF) World Championships have been held since 2004. Teams qualify for this event by finishing highly at various competitions. In 2006, more than 100 teams from eleven different countries competed in the event although, to date, it's the US teams who have, as they say, kicked serious butt.

----

3 Writer Jessica Bendinger's snappy high school cheerleading satire *Bring It On*, released in 2000, featured the following cheer: 'I'm sexy, I'm cute / I'm popular to boot / I'm bitchin', great hair / The boys all love to stare / I'm wanted, I'm hot / I'm everything you're not / I'm pretty, I'm cool / I dominate this school / Who am I? Just guess / Guys wanna touch my chest / I'm rockin', I smile / And many think I'm vile / I'm flying, I jump / You can look but don't you hump / I'm major, I roar / I swear I'm not a whore / We cheer and we lead / We act like we're on speed / Hate us 'cos we're beautiful / But we don't like you either / We're cheerleaders / We are cheerleaders!'

For millions of people around the world, a wheel of cheese is commonly placed on a cutting board with a small knife and a few crackers and nature is encouraged to take its course. In the English county of Gloucestershire, however, another use for a wheel of cheese has long been customary and that's as a kind of rolling lure in a hellbent downhill race that at times resembles a human avalanche.

As it has done for hundreds of years, cheese rolling takes place on the last Monday in May at Cooper's Hill in Gloucestershire. Once one of many activities of an unusual festival, which also included climbing the maypole, tug-of-war and shin-kicking,[1] cheese rolling became so popular that only it has stood the

---

1 Exactly as it sounds, shin-kicking is an activity whereby two people hold on to each other's shoulders and kick all hell out of each other's shins as they attempt to topple their opponent. Shin-kicking made its debut as a sport during the

test of time. While its origins are unknown, some have linked the event to when the ancient Romans had a fort atop Cooper's Hill. It's believed that the temperamental Romans often sent things hurtling down the hill's precipitous sides, though why they would have tossed out a wheel of cheese—and why anyone would have given chase, if indeed that ever happened—is anyone's guess.

As an activity, cheese rolling is both simple and dangerous; to some people a heady combination. With thousands of spectators, too sensible or too sober to take part, standing up and down each side of the long grassy slope, competitors in each of the day's four downhill races (three for men, one for women, twenty competitors in each race) gather at the top of the hill, which is so steep that from its summit the slope cannot always be seen. On the count of three a roller sets in motion a 7-pound wheel of Double Gloucester cheese. On the count of four the competitors are allowed to set off after it. Considering that due to the extreme steepness of the hill the cheese can reach speeds of 60 kilometres per hour, it is never actually caught unless, for some reason, it comes to rest. Consequently the person who wins the race is the one who first reaches the foot of the hill. Upon doing so she is then awarded a prize—the wheel of Double Gloucester.

Almost as soon as competitors start running down the hill (which is variously recorded to be 200–300 metres in length) all but the slowest lose their

---

inaugural Cotswold Olimpicks in 1612 (the Cotswolds are a range of hills in southwest England that take in a number of counties, including Gloucestershire). At its height of popularity it was a brutal sport where competitors (often miners) wore iron-capped boots, and sometimes clogs, in an attempt to maximize damage. Broken bones and shins stripped of flesh were not unusual injuries. Shin-kicking was outlawed in the mid 1800s but was resurrected for rural carnivals about 100 years later. These days competitors are not only forbidden to wear hard footwear but are also allowed to stuff their trouser legs with straw in order to cushion the blow.

footing; for not only is the hill steep but it also undulates, and its uneven surface is hidden by ankle-length grass. Inevitably many who stumble begin to cartwheel, like a rag doll thrown down an embankment from a moving car by a child bored out of her wits. Scrapes, bruises, strains, concussions and breaks are common, and first aid officials help fallen runners off the hill while others help catch competitors as they cross the line.

Even the spectators aren't necessarily safe. In 2005, an out-of-control Double Gloucester careened into the crowd and injured a spectator. Fortunately, the spectator—who presumably had never before been physically injured by a piece of cheese—inadvertently helped redirect the wheel on its merry way down the hill.

Other sports involving food

COMPETITIVE EATING

(see page 81)

FRUITCAKE TOSSING

Every January, Manitou Springs in Colorado, United States, hosts the Great Fruitcake Toss. Begun as a fun means of disposing of the kind of fruitcake you get given at Christmas that could be used to restump the house, the festival attracts hundreds of people eager to exercise their arm. If throwing fruitcake by hand isn't your thing, you can use the catapult supplied by the organizers.

ORANGE THROWING

Held annually in the alpine Italian town of Ivrea, the *Storico Carnevale di Ivrea* features an allegory rich in Vitamin C: that is, a three-day orange-throwing battle meant to represent a peaceful insurrection that took place in the Middle Ages, when poor families threw pots of beans into the street—beans that had been given to them by a feudal lord. One presumes the discarded beans didn't amount to a hill, hence the disrespect shown by the peasants. When the carnival first started it was common for revellers to throw pulses at each other for a bit of fun. Each to their own …

Oranges came to replace pulses in the 1930s and 1940s for speculative reasons. It's believed young girls watching the parade from their balconies used to lob oranges down on young men they had their eye on. Why they didn't just call out to them, or send them a text message, is a mystery. From the parade carriages the boys answered in kind and, over time, orange throwing became a big event during the carnival; despite the fact oranges are not grown in the region and have to be imported at considerable expense.

Today the contest is enacted in the town's main squares, where teams in carriages (representing the feudal lord's guards) battle against the nine orange-throwing teams on foot (representing the unhappy and rebellious commoners). The latter comprise hundreds of throwers, many of whom have strong throwing arms—hence the helmets and face grilles worn by the guards.

TOMATO FIGHTING

La Tomatina is the name of a festival held every August in the Spanish town of Buñol. Attracting tens of thousands of visitors, the highlight of *La Tomatina*—which began around 1945 for reasons no one is exactly sure of—is a mass tomato fight where more than 100 tonnes of over-ripe tomatoes are thrown at everyone and anyone. The only rules are that the tomatoes must be squished in the hand before being lobbed and no one is allowed to throw anything hard—like a brick, for example. The fight lasts about two hours before fire trucks come in to wash down the town's streets, which have come to resemble the killing floor at an abattoir.

WATERMELON-SEED SPITTING

The US town of Luling, Texas, is particularly proud of its melons and, as such, likes to show them off at an annual festival. The highlight of the Watermelon Thump, held every June since 1954, is the watermelon-seed spitting contest, which gets regular television coverage. Using only regulation watermelon seeds, the standing record is just over 68 feet. Melon-seed spitting is, as you'd expect, also the main event at the Melon Seed Spitting World Championships held every in the town of Fréchou in southwest France.

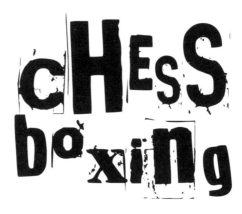

Considering a conceptual artist is credited with giving life to chess boxing, it's little wonder that at first glance this relatively new sport seems to make no sense whatsoever. As its name suggests, chess boxing is a hybrid of two sports that appear to be entirely incompatible. One requires you to challenge an opponent in a quiet, contemplative and cerebral battle of wits and strategy; the other requires you to repeatedly thump your opponent in the head and solar plexus.[1]

A chess-boxing match consists of eleven alternating rounds of chess and boxing, beginning with a 4-minute round of chess played on a table set up in

---

1 Such flippancy, of course, doesn't do boxing justice. While punching the head of an opponent is an important aspect of the so-called noble art, so too are speed, athleticism, fitness, tactical nous and a grim, unspoken acceptance that you may well end your career with the IQ of a lettuce.

the middle of a boxing ring. At the conclusion of the 4 minutes the chessboard and table are removed from the ring and the competitors don their gloves to begin a 2-minute round of boxing. When this round is complete the chessboard is brought back into the ring and the competitors remove their gloves for another 4-minute round of chess. This continues for a maximum of eleven rounds (six of chess, five of boxing). Wins are awarded by a knockout in the ring, a checkmate on the board, a boxing points decision or by exceeding the time limit in the chess rounds.[2]

While, in an ideal situation, both competitors are evenly matched both in and out of the ring, chess boxing creates the intriguing scenario where a competitor, realizing he is in dire trouble on the chessboard, enters the next round of boxing knowing his only chance of winning the match is to knock out his opponent. Similarly, a competitor realizing he is outgunned in the boxing ring must try to stay upright and quieten his ringing cerebellum long enough to finish off his opponent over the chessboard before the next boxing round begins. For such reasons the game's proponents consider chess boxing 'the thinking man's contact sport'. For exactly the same reasons others may consider the sport 'barmy'.

Cartoonist Enki Bilal first envisaged the idea of chess boxing in his 1992 graphic novel *Froid-Équateur* (*Cold Equator*). Then, in 2003, Berlin-based Dutch artist Iepe Rubingh, running with the idea that both chess and boxing are about controlled aggression, brought this concept to reality and staged a bout—in which he competed, and won—in a Berlin cultural centre. Since then Rubingh has established the World Chess Boxing Organization (whose

---

2 With a maximum total of 24 minutes devoted to chess, each player is allowed 12 minutes to deliberate over and complete his chess moves. When his 12 minutes expire the game is over. This prevents a player from simply using the chess rounds to rest ahead of the boxing rounds.

motto is 'Fighting is done in the ring and wars are waged on the board') which, in 2005, oversaw the creation of the first European chess-boxing title, won by Bulgarian chess pro Tihomir 'Tiger Tad' Titschko. Since then, chess-boxing gymnasiums have opened in Berlin and Cologne, in Germany, and the burgeoning sport has its sights set on the United States.

CLIFF diving

That most people would hesitate to jump off a 25-metre cliff into water—even if it were the only means of escaping a pack of angry boy bands—says much about the cliff divers who brave this kind of plummet voluntarily, often with only a swatch of Lycra for protection.

An offshoot of high diving, cliff diving is about striving for acrobatic perfection as divers fall at 90–100 kilometres per hour from a rock ledge (or human-made platform), which can be up to 28 metres above a body of water. The World High Diving Federation (WHDF) estimates that a bad water landing from a 26 metre-high ledge would be the equivalent of falling to the street from 13 metres. So it's perfectly understandable that many cliff divers, in addition to swimming briefs, also wear mouthguards. Anyone who has fallen onto bitumen from 13 metres has surely wished they'd been wearing a mouthguard at the time.

From the point of jumping to the point of impact with the water takes a diver approximately 3 seconds from the highest competition ledge (28 metres for men, 23 metres for women). This means there isn't a lot of time in which to admire the view. While the acrobatic manoeuvres the diver makes on his rapid descent are scored for competition purposes, the most crucial part of the dive is the entry.

Not only does a clean entry score high points but, better yet, it helps prevents serious injury since, at the point of impact, the parts of the diver's body under water are experiencing massive deceleration while the parts above it are still in full acceleration. A diver must be in peak condition and fully braced for impact, or risk emerging from the water needing to get the hems on all his trousers taken up.

Unlike Olympic high divers, whose highest jump is from the 10-metre platform, cliff divers tend to enter the water feet first, as this lessens the risk of serious head injury. In other ways the sports are similar. Like high divers, cliff divers also attempt to perform such acrobatics as pikes, somersaults and twists[1] as they fall. The dive's degree of difficulty is taken into account during scoring, along with the cleanness of the water entry. The best divers drop into

----

1　Dives are divided into six groups and three positions. The groups are: Forward—the diver faces forwards and rotates forwards; Backward—the diver faces backwards and rotates backwards; Reverse—the diver faces forwards and rotates backwards; Inward—the diver faces backwards and rotates forwards; Twisting—in executing any of the above, the diver performs a lateral, or sideways, twist; and Armstand—performed only from human-made platforms, armstand dives (dives that begin with a handstand) can be done forwards, backwards and reverse and may include twists.

　　Diving positions include: Straight—after jumping off the platform the diver keeps his whole body straight; Tuck—the diver bends at the hip and the knee, drawing his body into a ball before straightening into his descent; and Pike—the diver bends in half from the waist, keeping his legs and torso straight before straightening into his descent.

water like driven nails. The worst divers, like your overweight Uncle Kevin, slip in as elegantly as a refrigerator pushed off a bridge.

Cliff diving is said to have its roots in the late 1700s at Kaunolu in the Hawaiian Islands, where Kahekili, the king of Maui, was famous for *lele kawa* (cliff diving). Feeling particularly game one day, King Kahekili scaled a high promontory of volcanic cinder called Pu'u Keka'a, known today as Black Rock. With Pu'u Keka'a believed to be the site from which dead souls would leap into the afterlife, locals wouldn't touch it with a bargepole, let alone take the time to scale it and stand on its edge, tempting fate. But Kahekili was keen to demonstrate the size of his coconuts and plunged into the ocean below, emerging unscathed. In order to prove their courage and loyalty, Kahekili forced his warriors to follow his example and take the great leap off Black Rock—which today divides the beaches of Ka'anapali and Kahekili along a resort-lined stretch of coastline. A generation after Kahekili's reign, *lele kawa* competitions were being held, while these days King Kahekili's dive is re-enacted every evening for tourists.

Perhaps the most famous cliff diving in the world takes place in Acapulco, Mexico, a town that, between the 1940s and 1960s, was the epitome of cool and a hangout for the Hollywood jet set. Today the town's main tourist attraction is at La Quebrada where, watched by tourists who pay about US$3 a head, a troupe of hardy cliff divers hurl themselves—five times a day—off various points on a craggy cliff face, above a narrow, churning channel of seawater. While the local divers perform minimal acrobatics on the way down, they do have to coincide their 20–35 metre leap with an inrush of seawater to ensure there is enough water beneath them—water, of course, being a prerequisite of any successful dive. When the divers break the water fists first they are travelling at speeds close to 100 kilometres per hour.

Adding to the divers' risk is that the cliffs at La Quebrada do not overhang the water (unlike venues used in the WHDF world championships). This means that in addition to worrying about their entry into the water, divers also have to jump out far enough to clear the rocks— which are best described as jagged. If the Quebrada divers have an occupational health and safety officer (and that's doubtful) he, or she, should be sacked.

Something Similar

BRIDGE JUMPING

Stari Most (Old Bridge) is, or perhaps was, an elegant sixteenth century stone bridge in the beautiful city of Mostar, Bosnia and Herzegovina. Before it was destroyed by architecturally unappreciative Bosnian–Croat forces in 1993, the 29-metre-long semi-circular limestone structure hosted, for some 400 years, an annual competition in which young men would dive or jump from the pedestrian bridge into the testicle-shrinking waters of the Neretva River, some 21 metres below. As with many acts of bravery that resemble stupidity, jumpers were said to take part in order to prove themselves to their respective fiancées who, you would think, if they were really in love, would have talked them out of it on the grounds it was unnecessary, not to mention foolhardy.

In 2004, the bridge re-opened, having been painstakingly reconstructed in its original Ottoman style. Now a World Heritage site, the bridge is once again the venue for an annual diving competition attracting resilient locals, international divers and tens of thousands of spectators.

COMPETITIVE Eating

Though it's been going on at family dinner tables since time immemorial, competitive eating refers to organized and sometimes large-scale competitions during which amateur or, indeed, professional eaters attempt to eat as much food as possible in a short period of time. So frenzied and prodigious can the eating be that small children and pets would do well to keep clear of competitors—sometimes known as 'gurgitators'—lest they inadvertently wander into their feeding zone. Under the pressure of the clock and fellow competitors, discretionary eating is seldom practised.

Competitive eating has become so popular in the United States, in particular, that the activity, considered a sport by many, has a number of governing bodies; none bigger than the International Federation of Competitive Eating (IFOCE), which oversees about 100 'major league' eating events worldwide every year. Some IFOCE events, such as the elimination tournament called the US Open of Competitive Eating (which, fittingly, is sponsored by antacid manufacturer Alka-Seltzer), and the Fourth of July hotdog-eating contest at New York City's Coney Island, are televised by ESPN. Consequently, money is creeping into the sport and in 2006 IFOCE distributed about US$300,000 in prize money to its competitors. There is also a lucrative eating circuit in Japan.

Eating competitions, like eating competitors, come in many different forms. Most—which hark back to the kind of contests one might associate with a town fair or carnival—focus solely on a single foodstuff such as pies, meatballs, grilled-cheese sandwiches, hotdogs, doughnuts, cheesecakes, waffles, hamburgers or, commonly, any other food frowned upon by dieticians. Other times competitions tend to focus on the hosting town's local produce, be that watermelons, sweet potatoes or chilli peppers. Whatever the food, however, it seems there are always people willing to stuff it in their bellies in frightening amounts.[1]

Considering this, it may be presumed that the best competitive eaters physically resemble *Star Wars* villain Jabba the Hutt. This is not necessarily the case. Some of the world's leading gurgitators, such as Japan's Takeru 'Tsunami' Kobayashi (a six-time holder of the Coney Island world hot-dog eating record) and Korean-American Sonya 'The Black Widow' Thomas (who has eaten 552 oysters in a single sitting) are thin by anyone's estimation.[2] This seeming anomaly has prompted the 'belt of fat' theory, which postulates

----

1 The IFOCE is quick to remind impressionable members of the public that competitive eating should not be undertaken at home. IFOCE sanctioned events take place, it says, in a controlled environment with emergency medical staff present. Furthermore, the IFOCE is 'against at-home training' and 'strongly discourages younger individuals from eating for speed or quantity under any circumstances'. In short, step away from the cheesecake. You are not impressing anyone.

2 Another well-known female IFOCE competitor, Carlene LeFevre, is also slight. Most notable about her, however, is an eating manoeuvre she uses called 'the

that having large reserves of belly fat actually inhibits the expansion of the stomach when it's put under duress in an eating competition. Conversely, being thin allows the stomach to expand more readily. Thomas, for instance, weighs only 105 pounds. A top-four ranked eater on the IFOCE circuit, Thomas regularly outperforms men four times her size. Lest her success be attributed to a physical anomaly, doctors have told Thomas that her stomach is only slightly larger than normal.

The rules of competitive eating vary from tournament to tournament. Commonly, however, competitions are not open-ended, meaning that a strict time limit is given. Food that remains in a competitor's mouth when time expires will count towards the total, so long as it is swallowed. Finally, vomiting—known in the business as 'a reversal'—is permitted as long as it doesn't leave the competitor's mouth. Which could be said to defeat the purpose of vomiting in the first place.

---

pop' or 'popping'. In short, when she eats she bounces up and down, believing that it aids the downward journey and the compacting of the food, thereby allowing her to fit more in.

Some recent IFOCE records

Beef tongue (pickled):	3 lb 3 oz (1.45 kg) pickled beef tongue (whole) in 12 minutes (Dominic Cardo)
Cheesecake:	11 lb (4.99 kg) in 9 minutes (Sonya Thomas)
Chicken nuggets:	80 in 5 minutes (Sonya Thomas)
Cow brains:	57 (17 lb 11 oz/8.03 kg) in 15 minutes (Takeru Kobayashi)
Doughnuts (glazed):	49 in 8 minutes (Eric Booker)
Eggs (hard boiled):	65 in 6 minutes 40 seconds (Sonya Thomas)
French fries:	4 lb 7$\frac{1}{3}$ oz (2.02 kg) in 6 minutes (Cookie Jarvis)
Fruitcake:	4 lb 14$\frac{1}{4}$ oz (2.21 kg) in 10 minutes (Sonya Thomas)
Grilled cheese sandwiches:	47 in 10 minutes (Joey Chestnut)
Hamburgers (quarter-pounders):	11$\frac{1}{4}$ in 10 minutes (Don Lerman)
Hot dogs (including buns):	66 in 12 minutes (Joey Chestnut)
Ice cream (vanilla):	1 gal 9 oz (4.1 litres) in 12 minutes (Cookie Jarvis)
Jalapenos (pickled, short-form):	247 in 8 minutes (Richard LeFevre)

Mayonnaise:	4 x 32-oz bowls in 8 minutes (Oleg Zhornitskiy)
Meat pies:	16 x 6 oz pies in 10 minutes (Boyd Bulot)
Mince pies:	46 in 10 minutes (Sonya Thomas)
Oysters:	46 dozen (552) in 10 minutes (Sonya Thomas)
Pancakes (with bacon):	3$^1/_2$ lb (1.59 kg) in 12 minutes ('Crazy Legs' Conti)
Pasta (linguine):	6$^2/_3$ lb (3.02 kg) in 10 minutes (Cookie Jarvis)
Peas:	9$^1/_2$ x 1 lb (450 g) bowls in 12 minutes (Eric Booker)
Pork ribs:	8 lb 6$^1/_2$ oz (3.81 kg) in 12 minutes (Joey Chestnut)
SPAM:	6 lb (2.7kg) from the can in 12 minutes (Richard LeFevre)
Tacos:	48 soft chicken tacos in 11 minutes (Sonya Thomas)
Tiramisu:	4 lb (1.8 kg) in 6 minutes (Timothy Janus)
Watermelon:	13.22 lb (5.99 kg) in 15 minutes (Jim Reeves)

Conkers

Racier forms of entertainment have certainly blunted its appeal in recent times, but it's long been an autumn tradition in English schoolyards for young boys to show each other their nuts. That done, the boys take it in turns to propel their precious nut against the other boy's with the ultimate aim of breaking his to smithereens.

The game, of course, is conkers and the nuts are actually ripe seeds found inside the prickly casings shed by horse chestnut trees around September and October. Having scoured diligently though the autumn rustle for the biggest, hardest, most symmetrical nuts they can find (symmetry improves the integrity of a nut), prospective players prepare their arsenal for battle by boring a hole through each nut (with a skewer or drill) and threading a piece of string through the resulting hole.[1] With one end of the string knotted beneath the

---

1 It goes against the spirit of the game, but many boys look to artificially toughen their nuts by roasting them, soaking them in vinegar, or coating them in clear nail varnish. Two-time world conker champion Charlie Bray says on the World Conker Championships website (www.worldconkerchampionships.com) that the best

nut, and the other looped a couple of times around the palm, the modified nut—now a conker—becomes a kind of mini mace which tends to be swung in an overhand manner. The receiver, meantime, must dangle his conker submissively at a height chosen by the attacking player.

Being a mostly informal game—now played by girls as well as boys—the rules of conkers are changeable, with the only certainty being that smashing someone else's conker guarantees victory. Some schoolyards allow each player just one swing of his conker before his opponent gets a turn. Others allow three. Some award an extra swing to the first player to call 'strings' following an entanglement of conkers. Some award an additional swing if an opponent's conker is sent on a 360-degree loop (this is called a 'windmill' or 'round the world'), and others allow a conker that has fallen on the ground to be stamped on (and potentially broken) if the attacking player calls 'stampsies' before the defending player cries, somewhat ridiculously, 'no stampsies'.

Perhaps the most intriguing element to the game is the scoring system that rewards conkers that have accumulated days, months, even years of rigorous service. For instance, a brand new conker that hasn't seen battle is sometimes referred to as a 'one-er'. If a one-er defeats another one-er it becomes a two-er. If a one-er defeats a three-er it becomes a four-er. And so on. As this indicates, a conker's score or, perhaps more accurately, its worth, is increased by the worth of the conker it, well, conquers.[2] This creates the

----

underhanded way to harden a conker is to pass it through a pig. 'The conker will harden by soaking in its stomach juices. Then you search through the pig's waste to find the conker.' One might suggest that anyone who chooses such an unpleasant way to cheat should not be penalized but rewarded for their endeavour.

2 For many people, an untried conker is considered a 'none-er', not a one-er. For such people, a winning conker takes on the worth of an opposing conker plus one. Thus if a none-er beats another none-er it would become a one-er. If a one-er beats a two-er it would become a four-er, and so on.

scenario where champion conkers can embark on a generational reign of terror, kind of like Cliff Richard. Passed down between siblings like precious heirlooms, conkers can continue their merciless rule over the schoolyard for years. The fatal flaw in this system is that is requires honesty. But since boys are prone to boast about their nuts, the value of a conker can only be taken with a grain of salt. The conker itself, it should be noted, is inedible—grains of salt notwithstanding.

Since the worth and integrity of conkers will always be in doubt, the annual World Conker Championships[3]—held since 1965 in the town of Ashton in Northamptonshire, England—provides competitors with conkers. Men's, ladies', juniors' and teams' events are held, with all proceeds going to charity.

---

3 **The World Conker Championships Official Rules**
  - All conkers and laces are supplied by Ashton Conker Club. Laces must not be knotted further or tampered with.
  - The game will commence with a toss of a coin, the winner of the toss may elect to strike or receive.
  - A distance of no less than 8 inches or 20 centimetres of lace must be between knuckle and nut.
  - Each player then takes three alternate strikes at the opponent's conker.
  - Each attempted strike must be clearly aimed at the nut, no deliberate miss hits.
  - The game will be decided once one of the conkers is smashed.
  - A small piece of nut or skin remaining shall be judged out, it must be enough to mount an attack.
  - If both nuts smash at the same time then the match shall be replayed.
  - Any nut being knocked from the lace but not smashing may be re-threaded and the game continued.
  - A player causing a knotting of the laces (a snag) will be noted, three snags will lead to disqualification.
  - If a game lasts for more than 5 minutes then play will halt and the '5 minute rule' will come into effect. Each player will be allowed up to nine further strikes at their opponent's nut, again alternating three strikes each. If neither conker

Some other schoolyard games

BRANDINGS (OR BRANDY)

A simple, though potentially injurious activity, brandings is a group game whereby attacking players attempt to hit (and, ideally, 'brand') defenders by throwing a tennis ball at them. The game is played in an open space of any reasonable size and begins with one person being 'in'. When that person manages to hit another, both are then considered 'in' and can work together (by passing the tennis ball back and forth between them) in their attempts to brand more players. The game continues until the last person is branded. Rules vary but in one variation of the game players are allowed to defend themselves by deflecting the ball with their knuckles. Sometimes the game is played with a wet tennis ball, because it will leave an obvious mark on a target's clothing or body—and it hurts more.

has been smashed at the end of the nine strikes then the player who strikes the nut the most times during this period will be judged the winner.

NB. There are two stewards in charge of each game and their decision is final, except in the case of an unresolved query or dispute between Player and Steward, in which case the Chief Umpire will be called and his decision shall be absolutely final.

—From www.worldconkerchampionships.com

BRITISH BULLDOG

British bulldog (or bulldogs) is, to some, an overly rigorous tag-like game played mostly in the schoolyards of Britain, Australia and other Commonwealth countries. Due to its physical nature it is not unusual for schools to ban it. Consequently, it is very popular among schoolchildren.

Although the rules of British bulldog may vary from schoolyard to schoolyard, the game, best played on grass, begins with one person selected to stand in the middle of the playing area, who acts as a kind of defender (or bulldog) with everyone else down one end. On the bulldog's call, the main group rushes as one to the other side of the playing area. The bulldog attempts to tackle as many stampeding runners as she can, usually singling out a runner she is confident of catching. (This person is invariably identified by inch-thick glasses, a limp, or by the height of the waistband on his shorts or trousers.) Any runner tackled then becomes a bulldog himself.

Once all runners are either tackled or have made it to the other side of the playing area the bulldogs take stock, before the runners rush back across the playing area, once again trying to avoid the bulldogs. As the game wears on bulldogs soon outnumber the runners, and even the quickest, most agile runners cannot evade capture forever if the bulldogs work together. Often the last person caught becomes the initial bulldog for the next game.

One of the main variations of British bulldog is the means of converting runners to bulldogs. Traditionally a bulldog needs to tackle the runners to the ground rugby-style, or at least hold them up (or actually off the ground) for a pre-determined count, which is often 'British bulldog one, two, three'. In such variations children are often injured, with bruises and grazes common. Clothes and uniforms can also take a battering. For these reasons school authorities, not to mention many parents, look unfavourably upon the game.

A compromise version of the game, usually only played when there are authority figures in attendance, requires the bulldog to simply tag a runner. Like sugar-free soft drinks, this version of the game can often seem rather bland to a young child keen to explore both her physicality and her exciting ability to inflict pain on another human being.

ELASTICS

Traditionally a game played by girls—though many boys, perhaps showing their promise as sensitive men of the future, often join in—elastics combines athleticism with rhyme. Two girls stand facing each other inside a long loop of elastic, so it is taut at their ankles (which are wide apart so the elastic loop forms a rectangle). A third girl (or however many extra participants are up for the challenge) performs a series of hops and jumps over, inside and sometimes on the elastic while chanting the chosen rhyme. If she successfully negotiates the hops and jumps without getting tangled up, the elastic is lifted to the knees, then the thighs, then the waist, the difficulty of the task increasing each time.

FRENCH CRICKET

Just what the French part of this game's name is supposed to represent isn't
quite clear, for French cricket is a watered-down version of the English game
of cricket. Requiring no equipment, aside from a cricket bat (or tennis racket)
and ball, French cricket is a game for two or more players in which the legs of
the batsman (which, at all times, must remain together) double as the stumps.
A bowler, propelling the ball underarm, tries to hit the legs of the batsman
who, in turn, attempts to protect his legs and hit the ball (only an upward,
scooping-style stroke is permitted). If the ball hits the batsman's legs, or a
fielder catches a ball the batsman has hit on the full, he is 'out' and someone
else takes his place.

MARBLES

Most often played by children in schoolyards (although the self-proclaimed
World Marbles Championships are held annually in a West Sussex pub—
which isn't to say all participants necessarily imbibe), marbles is a game of
precision played with small glass, agate or steel balls.

One common version of the game is called 'ringer' and is played by two or
more players who kneel around a circle drawn in a bed of dirt or sand. Placing
a number of their marbles within the circle, players take position outside it
and, with the knuckles of their shooting hand stationary on the ground,
attempt to flick (with their thumb) a marble so that it knocks the opposition's
marble(s) out of the circle.

TETHERBALL

Predominantly a North American schoolyard game, tetherball is mainly played by primary school aged children or, stereotypically, teenagers who, in the cutthroat milieu of schools, might be classified under the genus *nerd*. Still, if this is indeed true, 'nerds' need exercise like everyone else and if playing tetherball is sneered at by the creatine-chomping athletic types with spanners for brains, the nerds will at least get the last laugh when they wind up running software companies and have to be awfully inventive to find ways to spend their wealth. That they played tetherball in their youth will be of little consequence.

Tetherball is simplicity on a stick. Its main feature is a 10-foot pole from which hangs (by some form of tether) a ball similar in size and weight to a volleyball. After one player serves the ball, by hitting it with a fist or palm, the game is on, with each of the players attempting to hit the ball past the other (if the server serves in a clockwise direction the receiver will have to hit in an anticlockwise direction or vice-versa) often enough so that the rope wraps completely around the pole causing the ball to hit the pole. When that happens the game is over. Since the server has a slight advantage, a best-of-three (or more) scenario is usually the norm.

To play fairly, the ball must not be hit twice per turn and it is poor sportsmanship to hit the ball down so that it windmills around the pole making it exceedingly difficult to return.

A similar game is tether tennis. This is played with a shorter pole, a tethered tennis ball and racquets. Most poles in this form of the game are topped with a coil of metal called a helical screw. The tether is attached to the screw and hitting the ball moves the tether up or down the screw. The game ends when the tether reaches the top or bottom of the screw.

COSTUMED football

Although it sounds almost pleasant and light-hearted, and just the sort of thing you might sign up for to give the kids a chuckle, historical (costumed) football—or *calcio storico Fiorentino*, as it is known in its hometown of Florence, Italy—appears to be as fun-filled as a full-blown riot in a maximum security prison.

Played every June or July, *calcio storico* is a Florentine tradition dating back to the 1500s. These days it is played to coincide with the celebration of St John's Day; St John the Baptist being not only the patron saint of Florence but, one can only presume, also the patron saint of grievous bodily harm.

Unofficially a mix of football (soccer), rugby, boxing and dress-ups, *calcio storico* is played on a large sand-covered pitch with slightly elevated goals running the width of each end. With twenty-seven players on each team the object of the game is to throw or propel the red-and-white-striped ball into the opposition's goal, scoring a *caccia* (or point) when successful. Other than that just about anything goes, meaning attempts to dispossess rival players of the ball more resemble muggings than tackling. Consequently, games have been known to get a little out of hand. In 2005 and 2006, for example, as many as ninety players came to the attention of police after a number of unsavoury incidents that brought to mind the opening sequence of Steven Spielberg's *Saving Private Ryan*. This resulted in the cancellation of the 2007 event, to allow simmering tensions to cool and court appointments to be met.

Calcio storico is contested by four teams representing the Florentine quarters: Santo Spirito, San Giovanni, Santa Maria Novella and Santa Croce. In a decision that made things considerably easier for future tourists, the quarters were, in the earliest days of *calcio storico*, assigned nicknames; respectively, *i Bianchi* (the whites), *i Verdi* (the greens), *i Rossi* (the reds), and *gli Azzurri* (the blues). Today, as then, the residents of each quarter support their team during *calcio storico* with genuine fervour,[1] adding much colour, and perhaps even a frisson of menace, to the event.

That said, if there's one thing that barely needs supplementing during *calcio storico* it's colour. Arguably the most distinctive thing about *calcio storico* is the pageantry surrounding the event and the traditional medieval costumes worn by players and officials. Before the games get underway there is a wonderful procession of participants and the city's nobles through the historic centre of Florence to the Piazza Santa Croce, where the games take place. On display are big, ornate flags, traditional drummers, armoured men on horseback, and

---

1 Naturally, when a fan's emotions get high, fervour can morph into mindless, though often satisfying, abuse. Chants heard during *calcio storico* include: *'Azzuri, Azzurri, vaffanculo!'* ('Blues, Blues, go fuck yourself!') and *'San Giovanni, San Giovanni, figli di puttane!'* ('San Giovanni, San Giovanni, sons of whores!'). While the sentiments in such chants are rather unpleasant they are, on the up side, very easy to learn.

columns of gnarled, teak-tough competitors with heads like concrete breeze blocks.

Finally, after being introduced to the expectant and, in some cases, rabid crowd, the players, many of them shirtless, take to the field in colourful pantaloons, which is perhaps the reason they appear to be so angry with the world and so willing to throw an errant elbow or two. Once the 50-minute match commences, brawls erupt all over the pitch like spot fires on a hot blustery day, as players look to hold each other off the ball, or stop rivals from supporting the ball-runner. At times it seems the progress of the ball comes second to getting square with a rival.

Every year, three matches are played on three separate days. The first two are qualifying matches (randomly drawn) with the winners meeting each other in a final played a week or so later—nowhere near enough time for broken noses, black eyes and grudges to mend. Although the winning team wins a mass of steaks equivalent in weight to the more traditional prize of a white calf, or *bistecca fiorentina* (which was historically butchered for the occasion—as if there hadn't been enough butchering going on already), the greatest prize is undoubtedly the glory they bring to their quarter for at least a year.

COW-CHIP throwing

It says something about a town that it is willing to promote itself as the 'cow chip capital of the world' and, as such, adopt as a kind of town emblem a caricature of a disc-shaped cow turd complete with eyes, a beaming, welcoming smile and a crown worn at a jaunty angle.[1] What that something might be is, of course, open to debate. On the one hand it suggests the residents of the US town of Beaver, Oklahoma, don't take themselves too seriously. On the other, it indicates there can't be a whole lot going on in downtown Beaver if cow manure and its aerodynamic potential are the carrot the town is dangling before the world.

Be that as it may, the former fur-trading post of Beaver has hosted the World Cow-Chip Throwing Championships for more than 30 years, which is more

---

1 The caricature is of 'King Cow Chip' and is reportedly a registered trademark. Now all the other towns around the world that want an anthropomorphized lump of manure as their emblem will have to tread very carefully, if you'll pardon the expression.

than a lot of other towns can put in their CV. Such longevity indicates the townsfolk are not the only ones who enjoy picking up, and giving temporary flight to, cow chips, meadow muffins, pasture patties, whatever you want to call them, and it's claimed people come from as far as Australia to compete.

Held every April at the Beaver County Fair, the chip throwing is as fair as you would hope. Organizers strive for equality by providing competitors with cow chips. This means that competitors from out of town do not have to transport their own manure from home in their carry-on luggage, something airlines presumably aren't too keen on due to manure's combustibility.[2] It also means there is some uniformity between chips, which can be no less than 6 inches in diameter.

The rules of cow-chip throwing are simple. Each competitor gets to select two chips from the chip wagon, which has an around-the-clock guard posted to prevent underhanded competitors from planting their own chips (that is, chips made by their own cows, not by the competitors themselves—that just wouldn't be right) so they can 'randomly' choose them later. Competitors may use any throwing technique they like, and styles vary from underhand, overhand, Frisbee and discus. The standing record is 185 feet 5 inches, achieved by Bobby Deevers in 2001.

Cow-chip throwing competitions are run in numerous other US states and in a few select countries such as Germany and Australia. Australia is also home to a related activity, most often conducted to raise money for charity, known as

---

2 It's been said that cow-chip throwing originated on the American frontier when settlers collected cow chips and threw them into their wagons to be used later as fuel (it's apparently odourless, soot free and produces good heat). Cows have been around a lot longer than that, however, and many cultures have long used cow manure as fuel. In India, and other countries, many still do. So it's difficult to believe cow chips weren't tossed around long before the American settlers decided to get their hands dirty.

'cow-pat bingo'. Usually held at a country fair, the game is played on a field marked up like a bingo card with numerous numbered squares drawn onto the grass. Tickets are sold to punters who bet on a particular square. A well-fed cow is then let loose and if nature takes its course on your particular square you go home a winner.

Other throwing events

WELLINGTON WANGING

Wellington boots, or 'Wellies', are heavy rubber boots commonly worn by farm workers, fishmongers, and children whose parents are sick and tired of them stomping through mud and puddles in their shoes and socks. Residents from England, Finland, Australia and New Zealand are particularly partial to throwing 'wellies', or gumboots, for distance. The town of Taihape on the North Island of New Zealand is so fond of the practice (boots tend to be gripped at the top of the throat prior to throwing) it calls itself the 'gumboot throwing capital of New Zealand' and holds a Wellington-wanging competition every 'Gumboot Day', the first Tuesday after Easter.

EGG THROWING

One of the many activities offered every June at Swaton Vintage Day in Lincolnshire, England, is the so-called 'World Egg Throwing Championship', an event overseen by the august World Egg Throwing Federation. Four disciplines usually feature in the championship: egg throwing and catching; egg relay; egg throwing for distance; and egg throwing for accuracy. The crowd pleaser is the throwing and catching event because it is the riskiest. It's an event for teams of two with the winners being the team who can throw and catch an uncooked egg (without breaking it, of course) the farthest. It's believed that the world record for egg throwing and catching was set in Jewett, Texas, in November 1978 when Johnie Dell Foley threw a fresh egg an astonishing 323 feet 2 inches before it was cleanly caught by his cousin, Keith Thomas.

MOBILE PHONE THROWING

In Scandinavia, mobile phone throwing has developed from a satisfying— though very much personal—activity to a major event. Well, at least in Savonlinna, Finland. There the annual Mobile Phone Throwing World Championships have been held since 2000. Unfortunately for prospective throwers who would like to show their own recalcitrant mobile phones who's boss in front of hundreds of spectators, only phones provided by the organizers may be thrown. A number of throwing categories exist, such as 'original' (where an overarm action is used—one throw per competitor only—and distance is the only thing that matters) and 'freestyle', where throwers will be judged on the aesthetics of their run-up and release. Various places, including the United Kingdom, Switzerland, Germany and the Netherlands, have national titles.

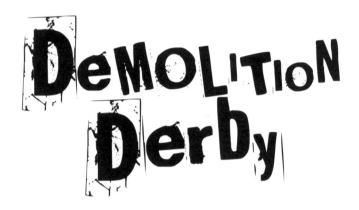

DEMOLITION Derby

Resembling both the streets of Bangkok and the fantasy some people have when bullied by their fellow motorists in heavy traffic, a demolition derby is a dramatic motor sport where competitors deliberately crash their cars into each other's vehicles until only one car remains operational.

As satisfying as that may sound, demolition derbies are inherently dangerous and, as such, a number of safety directives and measures are commonly observed; one being that the driver's-side door of a vehicle must not be deliberately rammed. To assist competitors in avoiding this crucial area, the driver's door must be painted in a contrasting colour to the rest of the car. This may not be as helpful as it first appears, since demolition derby vehicles tend to ram each other in reverse, as this protects their engines and front-wheel-drive systems.

Demolition derby vehicles are not usually in the kind of condition that would catch your average motorist's eye on a showroom floor. All glass is removed, doors are welded shut, bumper bars are shortened, batteries and petrol tanks are relocated away from the extremities and all interior features (including additional seats, plastic trim, CD players and, yes, even cup holders) are jettisoned. In short, the cars are unadorned hunks of metal usually purchased from a wrecker. Not that this matters, as demolition derby vehicles don't tend to survive more than one derby.

Unlike banger races,[1] demolition derbies tend to take place on dirt fields, which are watered before competition. The resulting mud adds an element of unpredictability. It also keeps the speed of vehicles down, improving the safety of drivers.

Demolition derbies first became popular in the United States in the 1950s when, popular opinion has it, the times were as inoffensive and routinely wholesome as Richie Cunningham[2] (notwithstanding the Communist witch-hunts going on at the time in Washington DC). Perhaps as a result, the birth of a seemingly subversive sport was all but inevitable. However, as demolition derbies were both intended to be, and ultimately taken as, a bit of a laugh, it didn't actually turn out to be all that shocking, let alone subversive, after all.

----

1   Banger races are a British variation of the demolition derby wherein vehicles balance wanton destruction with racing (around a dirt racetrack usually oval-shaped, sometimes figure-eight-shaped). Just to make things more difficult, more absurd, and, presumably, more entertaining, some banger races feature cars towing caravans.

2   Richie Cunningham, played by actor-cum-film-director Ron Howard, was a nice, clean-cut character in the American sitcom *Happy Days*—which was made in the 1970s but pictured life in the 1950s. As it happens, a demolition derby once featured in a *Happy Days* storyline because resident tough Arthur 'Fonzie' Fonzarelli had an on-again-off-again thing with a professional demolition derby driver called Pinky Tuscadero. Although Fonzie consistently wore leather and was inordinately neat, it should be pointed out that, being the 1950s, there was nothing ground-breaking about their relationship. Pinky was, in fact, a woman.

During the 1950s, 1960s and 1970s, cars used in demolition derbies were huge, steel American-made beasts. But as these cars became harder to come by, European and Japanese-style mid- and compact-sized cars were, and are, more commonly used. Though such cars are thought to be less safe than their bigger precursors—which didn't tend to crumble as easily as a modern car, as anyone who has received a $1000 bodywork bill after colliding with a moth will know—they provide derby fans considerable entertainment, as their protected front-wheel-drive systems can often allow them to remain in a derby even when they look like crushed cans.

Inevitably, as familiarity set in, demolition derbies embraced different kinds of vehicle type, such as minivans, school buses, ride-on lawnmowers and even combine harvesters. Every year in Lind, Washington, for instance, a combine harvester demolition derby takes place, featuring machines way past their usefulness in the field. As tough as tungsten and the size of buses, combine harvesters ploughing into each other would be even more spectacular than it sounds were it not for the fact the behemoths of the field aren't exactly greased lightning.

Another spin-off demolition-style event is a rollover competition. Rather than attempting to wreck an opponent's vehicle, a rollover driver strives to total his own as spectacularly as possible. To do this, the driver aims his speeding heap at a ramp, but instead of going over it on all four wheels he attempts to hit the ramp with only the wheels on one side of his vehicle. That done it only takes a small, deliberate shift of the steering wheel to make the car roll over—hopefully, more than once.

One presumes that the driver who rolls his car the greatest number of times is declared the winner—and that his winning cheque is then mailed to his widow.

DOG Sledding

Dog sled racing, or dog sledding, is primarily a winter sport. A team of dogs pulls a sleigh-like contraption on the rear rails of which stands a driver, known as a musher. Dog sledding takes place across and through snowbound tundra, spruce forests and mountain ranges (wheeled sleds are sometimes used for races over dirt and mud), and the dogs used, known as sled dogs, are especially suited for the purpose; long of limb, thick of fur and stout of heart. In short, not at all the kind of dog that would need a lie-down on the way to the corner shop for some milk, and certainly not one that would be seen dead in a natty little woollen vest onto which its name is embroidered.

Particularly popular in Canada, Alaska, and northern Europe, dog sledding is contested over distances varying from a few kilometres to 1151-mile epics like Alaska's Iditarod (see page 106). Races are further differentiated by the size of the dog team, with anything from three to twelve dogs per team common—although some races involve teams of up to twenty-four dogs, which is a lot of tummies to be scratched and a lot of dishes to be filled at the end of a day's racing. Generally, dog sled races begin with staggered starts (meaning teams set off at timed intervals), although mass starts, which resemble feeding time at the pound, are also popular.

A musher and sled are vital components of any dog sled team, but the stars of the show are, naturally, the dogs. While many different dog breeds can be used in dog sledding, sled dogs are traditionally Alaskan Malamutes and Siberian Huskies—breeds that have long been used by native peoples in Alaska and Siberia for herding and transporting loads across country. Good sled dogs are strong, as well as being capable of travelling great distances while maintaining high speeds (sled dogs average 20–32 kilometres per hour over distances of up to 40 kilometres). They actually prefer cold, snowy weather, as it's softer on the pads of their feet and helps keep them cool when working.

Modern sled dogs are hitched in pairs, with each pair hitched to a tugline that, in turn, is attached to a central gangline that runs through the pack to the musher.

The Iditarod

The Iditarod Trail Sled Dog Race is a 1151-mile race held annually in Alaska since 1973. Considered the toughest dog sledding race in the world, the Iditarod, which allows teams of no more than sixteen dogs, often takes

----

place in the kind of conditions that would have your average polar bear calling in sick: blizzards, high winds, and temperatures which, factoring in wind chill, can drop to minus 60 degrees Celsius. Though their thick fur inures them to such cold, sled dogs competing in the Iditarod tend to wear booties to help protect their feet against the harshness of ice and rocks.

The race is considered a link to both the early settlers and Native Alaskans.[1] The latter used dog sleds for transport and commerce, and are believed to have used parts of the trail hundreds of years before Russian fur traders arrived in the 1800s. After that, dog sleds became the main means of delivering mail and supplies to, and between, trading posts and settlements

----

----

1 Some erroneously believe that the Iditarod was started to commemorate what became known as the 'Great Race of Mercy': the 1925 serum run to Nome. The 'Great Race' concerns a mercy dash to deliver antitoxin from Anchorage to Nome, where a diphtheria epidemic threatened locals, in particular Inuit children. With all planes out of action it was decided to transport the 9-kilogram cylinder of serum by train to Nenana, some 480 kilometres away. From there the serum was transported another 1085 kilometres to Nome by a relay of twenty mushers and more than 100 sled dogs. The serum arrived in Nome on February 2, just five and a half days after it left Anchorage. The musher who brought the serum into Nome was Norwegian Gunnar Kaasen who, along with his lead dog, Balto, became something of a celebrity. Considering that a statue of Balto was erected in Central Park in New York City soon after, it could be argued that his fame outstretched that of his human partner. Perhaps a little hard done by (though presumably no one participated to become popular) were Leonhard Seppala and his lead dog, Togo, who are widely thought to have transported the serum through the most hazardous stretch of the route.

----

across the Alaskan interior during the cold dead of winter. While planes and snowmobiles came to marginalize dog sledding as a transport option, it has always persisted as a much-loved and deeply respected recreation and sport.[2]

For ceremonial purposes, the Iditarod starts every year in Anchorage, although the official start to the race takes place a day later in Wasilla, in south-central Alaska (the 80-kilometre route between Wasilla and Anchorage counts but the times don't, meaning mushers can take in the scenery until racing starts in earnest the following day). The trail continues up the Rainy Pass of the Alaska Range and into the mostly deserted Alaskan interior before turning left to run along the shore of the Bering Sea. The end point is at Nome in western Alaska. The route takes mushers and their mutts through the fringes of urban centres, small Athabaskan and Inuit settlements, and through the vastness of Alaska's wilderness.

Awarding a total of US$800,000 in prizes, the Iditarod is broken up into twenty-six or twenty-seven stages (depending whether the race takes the

----

---

2 As with almost all sports involving animals, dog sledding has attracted disapproval from some animal welfare campaigners who claim that in addition to the physical strain of racing (it's not unheard of for dogs to die during an Iditarod), sled dogs can be pushed too hard for too long. Moreover, critics contend that the confined kennelling of many sled dogs is detrimental to their health. Dog sledding advocates claim their dogs are much loved, well looked after and that they are bred specifically for racing and pulling. They also point to the Iditarod's strict animal welfare guidelines, which involve thorough pre-race veterinary checking, as well as interval checking during the race.

---

northern or southern route) of varying lengths. At the end of each stage is a checkpoint where mushers must sign in and where any supplies they pre-purchased in Anchorage are available to them (including food, booties for the dogs and camping gear). It's mandatory, however, for mushers to carry certain supplies, such as a sleeping bag, snowshoes, an operational cooker, enough fuel to bring three gallons of water to the boil and eight booties for each dog. It's also compulsory for them to make at least three stops during the race: one 24-hour stop and two others of eight hours each.

As with most sports over the years, winning times have steadily dropped. In winning the inaugural Iditarod, Dick Wilmarth and his team of dogs took a touch over 20 days to complete the journey. In 2002, however, winner Martin Buser recorded the fastest ever time: 8 days, 22 hours, 46 minutes and 2 seconds. If that time seems unnecessarily precise considering the length of the race, it should be mentioned that in 1978 Dick Mackey's winning margin was just 1 second. However, the result was mired in controversy, since second place-getter Rick Swenson physically crossed the finish line first. But, crucially, Mackey's lead dog crossed the line a second before Swenson's. Winning by a nose. Literally.[3]

---

3 Swenson, at least, would go on to have his day in the sun. He holds a record five
   Iditarod titles to his name, the first in 1982. And lest the Iditarod appear like a
   boys' club, one of the most successful mushers of all time is four-time winner
   Susan Butcher. Other famous Iditarod women include Mary Shields (who in 1974
   became the first woman to complete the race) and Libby Riddles (who in 1985
   became the first woman to win the race).

The traditional equipment list for the curious game of dwile flonking suggests its place in the pantheon of world sports lies somewhere in the darkest reaches of the pantheon's broom cupboard: a bucket of ale; an accordion; a rag soaked in beer (the dwile); a stick with which to fling the dwile (the driveller); and a collection of rural English couture, such as pork pie hats and collarless shirts.

Played between two teams of twelve, one of which starts the game 'batting', the other 'fielding', dwile flonking resembles the kind of game drunk cricketers would come up with if left overnight to their own devices in a Cornwall inn. The game begins with the fielding team holding hands and forming a circle (called a girter) around a member of the batting side (called a flonker). Once everyone is in formation, an onlooker, who with any luck isn't tone deaf, plays the accordion.[1] At the commencement of the music, the girter moves in a circle around the flonker, who, while holding the 60-centimetre driveller (on the end of which is the dripping dwile), turns in the opposite direction to the girter. Finally, when the music mercifully stops without notice, the flonker attempts to hit members of the girter by flinging the dwile at them.

Quite clearly, much satisfaction is to be gained by the flonker if he hits someone in the girter with the cold, beer-soaked rag. Almost as satisfying are the points to be gained, with three for a face hit, two for a torso hit and one for a limb hit. It's when the flonker misses, however, that the game *really* gets interesting. Under some varieties of dwile flonking, the flonker who has missed all targets after two turns must drink a pot of ale—either from the bar or, disturbingly, from the bucket he's been using to wet the dwile—before the girter, now forming a straight line, can pass the dwile from one end of the line to the other.

Points accumulate until all the members of the batting side have 'flonked' (batted), after which the teams swap roles. As in Test cricket, both teams get two turns at bat. Providing anyone is sober enough to keep score (highly unlikely), the winning team is the one that accrued the most points. Naturally, the losing side is too drunk to care.

Just when this glorified drinking game was invented is something of a mystery. One theory says it's a traditional game harking back to medieval times, while another links it to a couple of Suffolk printers—who obviously had a penchant for slapstick—in 1966. Be that as it may, 'dwile' is a real word (a Suffolk dialect term for a dishcloth) with similarities to the Dutch word

---

1 What he plays is entirely optional although, undoubtedly, it will be annoying. This says more about the nature of accordions than it necessarily does about accordion players.

for a floorcloth, *dweil*. Since there were links between East Anglia and the
Netherlands during the eighteenth century, it's possible that the Suffolk dialect
word was borrowed from the Dutch.

Some other pub games

AUNT SALLY

Played almost exclusively in Oxfordshire, England, Aunt Sally is a one-on-one
or team game where players throw 18-inch-long batons at a short, squat
wooden skittle, known as a doll. Standing anywhere from 10–30 feet away,
competitors attempt to knock the doll off a swivelling stake without hitting the
stake itself. The doll was originally a figurine of an old woman and the term
'Aunt Sally' is now used figuratively to mean something that is a target for
criticism. Women named Sally who also happen to be aunts are advised not to
take this to heart.

DEVIL AMONG THE TAILORS

A form of table skittles, Devil Among the Tailors requires a specially made
table-top box in which nine small skittles stand arranged in a three-by-three
formation. On one corner of the shallow-edged box stands a wooden post
from which hangs a small wooden ball. The aim of this English pub game is to

----

knock down as many skittles as possible by swinging the ball around the post (rather than directly at the skittles) so that it resembles a wrecking ball operated by a driver who clearly had a longer lunch than he was meant to.

RINGING THE BULL

Ringing the Bull challenges players to swing a bull's nose-ring that is dangling from the ceiling on a piece of string, onto a metal hook on a wall. Played in some English watering holes, a variation of the game is also played in and around the Caribbean.

SUMO WRESTLING

A relatively new activity, pub sumo wrestling is based loosely and irreverently on actual sumo wrestling—the ceremonial Japanese sport where mostly enormous men in G-string-style traditional costumes try to knock each other out of a circular platform using power and leverage over striking, which is not allowed. Since very few pub goers have what it takes to be authentic sumo wrestlers (prodigious beer guts, though prolific in pubs, are not really enough), some enterprising publicans helpfully fit them out in enormous, inflatable sumo suits. When sufficiently drunk, pub goers step into these cumbersome suits and attempt to bump their rival out of the fighting circle without falling over themselves. Unlike real sumo wrestling, pub sumo welcomes female competitors.

TOAD IN THE HOLE

Toad in the Hole involves throwing brass discs ('toads') from about 8 feet at a hole in a large box. Two points are scored for dropping a toad into the hole, one point is scored for landing a toad on the box top. Some have suggested the game, which is linked to Tudor England (around the 1500s), has enjoyed a resurgence of late because the Lewes Town Hall in East Sussex hosted the 2006 and 2007 World Championships.

VELCRO WALL

A modern activity available at some pubs and fun fairs, this is a suitably silly game in which enthusiasts slip into a jumpsuit adorned with Velcro, then run towards, and leap as high as they can onto, a wall also covered with Velcro. The purpose of the game is for contestants to stick themselves as high on the wall as possible, which requires making contact with the wall with as much bodily surface area as possible. Usually the runway is equipped with a mini trampoline, while the hard edges and surfaces in the immediate vicinity are covered in inflatable barriers to protect participants from injury.

Like polo, except using elephants instead of horses, this sport is just the sort of thing you could imagine was created by a couple of men in a bar. It comes as no surprise, then, to discover that elephant polo *was* created by a couple of men in a bar.[1]

The presumably well-lubricated meeting in a St Moritz watering hole between James Manclark, a Scottish landowner and former Olympic tobogganer, and Jim Edwards, owner of a jungle lodge in Nepal, led to the creation in 1982 of the World Elephant Polo Association (WEPA). Soon after, WEPA oversaw its first games of elephant polo, played on a grass airfield in Meghauly, which is located on the edge of the Royal Chitwan National Park in southern Nepal.[2]

---

1 Pure speculation imagines the Eureka moment went something like this: 'Dude! I've got two words for you ... *Elephant. Polo.*'

2 Manclark and Edwards initiated elephant polo in its current guise but they were not the creators of the game. One theory holds that members of the then

Every December since then, WEPA has hosted an invitational tournament with many players coming from a variety of countries to take part, although they tend to form teams that represent particular sponsors, rather than nations. Elephant polo is also played in India, Sri Lanka and Thailand, which is home to the King's Cup tournament in Hua Hin.

Like polo, elephant polo is a team game played on a rectangular pitch in which the object is to score the most goals by hitting the ball through the opposition's goalmouth, a set of posts set about 8 yards apart and centred at each end of the field. Teams of three or four players take to the pitch (during two 7–10 minute periods, or chukkas). Each team member shares her elephant with a *mahout* (or driver), a skilled trainer who also works with and drives the elephants during their 9 to 5 jobs taking tourists out on safaris. Prior to the tournament, a *mahout* is assigned to a particular elephant and will stay as the driver of that elephant no matter what team it is assigned to.[3]

The first elephant polo games were played with a football (soccer ball). However, it was quickly discovered that footballs were far from ideal since the elephants appeared to enjoy turning them into pancakes, which may or may not have been the pachyderms' way of saying they'd rather be doing something else. Nowadays, elephant polo is played with a standard polo ball (a hard plastic ball about 8 centimetres in diameter). The players use mallets that

---

Maharajah's harem first played elephant polo in India, in the late 1800s. Another credits the India-based British aristocracy of the same period with creating the game—surely as a quirky amusement.

3 In the interests of fairness, the sixteen or so elephants used during the WEPA tournament form a talent pool from which all the teams draw. Players swap elephants and their drivers between matches, and even during half-time. This increases the communication difficulties on the pitch since it is the driver's responsibility to instruct the *mahout* where to position the elephant on the field. Exacerbating the problem is that most of the *mahouts*, and all of the elephants, only understand Nepali.

vary in length depending on the height of the elephants. Mallets ranging from 1.5 metres to 3.6 metres in length are common.

Most of the sport's rules are based on those of horse polo, although there are a few notable differences. For one, the elephant polo pitch measures about 100 metres by 70 metres (as opposed to polo's 275 metres by 180 metres), as a concession to the slower speed and lesser mobility of the elephant. For another, elephants are not allowed to lie down and cover the goalmouth, and should they do so the team in question is penalized. Other penalties are incurred if an elephant picks the ball up with its trunk and if an elephant steps on the ball. For this reason it's vital that all participating elephants thoroughly read the rules before taking to the field.

Other polo variations

As a game played with mallets and a ball in which the object is to score in the opposition's goal, polo has spawned many variations—bearing in mind that some sports that use the word 'polo', such as water polo and canoe polo, have little in common with horse polo and, as a result, can hardly count as a variation. Some polo variations include:

YAK POLO

Played on yaks instead of horseback, yak polo— created as a tourist attraction in the early 2000s—is played seasonally in Mongolia. Though a

---

temperamental animal, yaks have the advantage of sure footing and can play on any surface, including ice. This sport-cum-tourist attraction is, reportedly, mainly run by nomadic herders.

Mongolia, like India, is also partial to a spot of camel polo, another game created around the tourist industry.

BICYCLE POLO

An outdoor game in which bicycles replace horses, bicycle polo is played on a rectangular grass field measuring approximately 150 metres by 100 metres, although field size can vary dramatically. According to the International Bicycle Polo Federation, Irishman Richard Mecredy invented the game in 1891. The first international match was played as long ago as 1901, when Ireland beat England 10–5. Bicycle polo was an Olympic demonstration event in the 1908 London Olympic Games, with Ireland beating Germany to the gold medal.

In bicycle polo, cyclists use metre-long mallets and a polo ball. Four players on each team can be on the field at any one time and the game lasts four chukkas of at least $7^{1}/_{2}$ minutes each.

The sport's halcyon days were the in 1930s, but bicycle polo is still played in a dozen or so countries, and a nominal world championship is held annually, although at most half a dozen countries contest it. The sport is particularly popular in India and the United States, where the governing bodies are, respectively, the Cycle Polo Federation of India and the Bicycle Polo Association of America.

SEGWAY POLO

Played by a small number of enthusiasts in the United States and elsewhere (the San Francisco-based Bay Area Segway Enthusiasts Group were one of the earliest to play the sport), Segway polo is not exactly a sport that's got the world mesmerized. The reason for this is that, naturally, to play the game each player requires a Segway, an electric-powered, two-wheeled, self-balancing transportation device in which users lean forward to move forward, and lean back to move backwards. If the environmentally-friendly Segway—sometimes used by criminally unfit and self-important shopping centre security guards—becomes a major form of transportation in years to come, one might expect a whole range of Segway-related activities to increase in popularity, not least Segway polo which, unlike polo played with animals, produces no noxious piles that need shovelling.

Though its rules are simple and its required equipment could be purchased from a hardware store for the kind of loose change you might find in the toe of someone else's shoe while they are swimming, flags is a game played almost exclusively by one group of people: surf lifesavers. Just why this is the case is something of a mystery, but it may have a little to do with the average beachgoer's belief that to exercise on a beach defeats the whole purpose of being there in the first place.

Flags is one of many games contested by surf lifesavers in Australia, New Zealand and South Africa in order to sharpen their reflexes, so that they can respond quickly when called into action (see page 122). The game, played by men, women and children (known in surf lifesaving circles as 'nippers'), can be contested by any number of competitors, who begin proceedings by lying side-by-side, belly down on the sand, with one hand on top of the other and their toes resting on a line drawn across the soft sand. In a parallel line about

20 metres behind them are a number of 30-centimetre-long baton-like rubber hoses, called flags, pushed into the sand. Crucially, there is one less flag than the number of competitors.

At first, lying there in the sand, the competitors have their heads raised, as if startled by someone rummaging through their bags. But out of their line of vision a starter calls 'heads down' and the competitors must drop their chins to their hands in the manner of someone who's got a stomach full of hot chips and is about to sleep it off, potential sunburn be damned. Moments later the starter blows a whistle and the race in on—with competitors rising from the sand and swivelling in one motion before running desperately towards the flags, mindful not to obstruct a fellow competitor. Considering the relatively short distance to run, flags races usually end with competitors diving full length to secure a flag. Anyone even remotely versed in mathematics will realize this means one of the competitors will be left empty-handed when the storm of sand has settled.

From this point, the game continues with the competitor who failed to secure a flag eliminated, á la musical chairs—admittedly a less strenuous game and one where players aren't normally half undressed. The remaining competitors go back to the start line while, again, one flag less the number of competitors is placed in the sand. Eventually, after a series of eliminations, only two competitors remain and both are chasing a single flag. The person who grabs that flag is the winner and, in all likelihood, the person who'll find the most sand in the gusset of her swimwear. Fortunately, the ocean is close at hand.

Other Surf Sports

Surf lifesaving clubs[1] regularly hold inter- and intra-club surf lifesaving carnivals in which members compete against each other in a range of beach and water events. With the advent of inflatable rescue boats, many of the rescue implements and techniques used in competition are seldom used in real-life situations, but, for reasons of tradition, are still contested at carnivals. These include:

SURFBOAT

Surfboats are four-oar-driven boats that accommodate five crew (there are separate races for male and female crew); one at each oar and one, a 'sweep', who stands at the rear and operates another oar as a rudder. The long, almost almond-shaped boats are designed to negotiate big surf. They can slide sideways, however, particularly when approaching shore, thus presenting an easy target for a wave. Though dangerous and decidedly

---

1 Surf lifesaving clubs originated in the early 1900s when it was realized that not everyone who went for a dip in Sydney's many beaches made it safely back to their towel. This happened shortly after the law prohibiting daylight bathing— established for reasons of modesty—was relaxed. As a result of the influx of people to beaches, volunteers were trained in the art of rescue and resuscitation, and located at specific beaches, to respond to people in distress. Unfortunately, in an unforeseen consequence, the lifesaving movement would eventually spawn *Baywatch* and unleash David Hasselhoff and Pamela Anderson on an unsuspecting world.

unpleasant for the crew, a surfboat overturned in rough surf is a spectacular sight for onlookers.

Surfboat competitions begin with the boat floating in knee-deep water and the crew standing beside it. On the starter's order the crew board the boat and row it through the breakers to a buoy stationed at least 400 metres from shore. The boats must then round their respective turning buoy and return to the beach.

Surfboats are regularly raced at lifesaving carnivals but they are seldom, if ever, used for rescues, which may be just as well as it's common for men in surfboats to combat chafing by pulling their briefs-style swimming trunks up their backsides so they form a disquieting wedge. Though undoubtedly delighted to be rescued, one might imagine that's the last thing a distraught, half-drowned swimmer needs to see.

IRB

Inflatable rescue boats (IRBs) are commonly used for surf rescues. IRB competitions are also a staple event at surf carnivals, and involve a crew of two (a driver and a crew person) who begin by pulling the IRB along the sand and into the water then break through the surf to reach a third team-member playing the role of a swimmer in distress. In the basic rescue discipline, the IRB needs to be driven about 140 metres from shore and pulled up beside the patient, with the crew member hauling her in as quickly as possible so the IRB can speed back to shore. (It's important the driver and crew member don't allow the boat's propeller to cut the living daylights out of the patient—an eventuality that could be described, from the patient's perspective, as out of the frying pan and into the fire.) As the IRB hits the shore the driver must kill the engine, leap out of the boat and race a short distance over the sand to the finish line.

SURF SKI

Flat, open-water, one- or two-person crafts powered by a competitor using a double-bladed paddle, surf skis are regularly raced in carnivals. Competitors typically begin the race standing in knee-deep water with the long (about 6 metre) craft beside them. At the starter's gun they board the ski and attempt to build momentum as quickly as possible. Though fast through the water, surf skis are as unstable as Argentina's economy and competitors often have great difficulty negotiating them through a strong swell. Once they manage to do that, however, they reach their respective turning buoy before heading back to shore. Ski races vary greatly in distance, from several hundred metres to ultra-marathon events of up to 240 kilometres, such as occurs every two years in South Africa, where competitors race between Port Elizabeth and East London.

BOARD

Lifesavers use large fibreglass boards—not designed for standing on, unlike surfboards—as an alternative means to swimming when conducting a rescue. By lying face down, a lifesaver can use her arms as paddles and then use the board itself as a kind of floating stretcher once she reaches a patient. Surf carnivals feature board races of varying distances, starting and ending on the sand, with buoys used as turning markers. It's a popular discipline for nippers.

IRONMAN

Although the term 'Ironman' is a registered trademark used to describe long-distance triathlons sanctioned by the World Triathlon Corporation,[2] the term has been used by surf lifesaving since the 1960s to describe a multi-discipline surf race comprising swimming, board-paddling, surf-ski-paddling and running, in that order. Race distances vary, with one of the longest being the Coolangatta Gold, held annually between Surfers Paradise and Coolangatta in Queensland. This gruelling race involves a 23-kilometre ski, 650-metre run, 3.5-kilometre swim, 4-kilometre run, 5.5-kilometre board paddle and finishes with a 10-kilometre run.

2   The Ironman refers to a triathlon race of a specific, mind-and-body-destroying distance: a 3.86 kilometre swim, 180.2 kilometre bicycle ride and a 42.195 kilometre marathon run. The most famous Ironman race is the Ironman World Championship, held annually in Hawaii since 1978. If the distances don't make it difficult enough, the baking heat and wind crank up the discomfort level. Even the elite of the elite will take eight (men) or nine (women) hours to finish the race. Seventeen hours is considered the cut-off time, which means the lights will be out when you cross the line and you won't be considered an official finisher, which isn't exactly what you want to discover considering what you've just put yourself through.

Freediving

Broadly encompassing a number of underwater activities in which participants forgo breathing apparatus, freediving popularly refers to the practice of diving to achieve either great depths, distances or times on a single breath of air.

Also known as competitive apnoea (which sounds like just the sort of thing that would go on at a male-only sleep disorder clinic[1]), freediving is considered an extreme sport. It's a description particularly apt for divers whose objective is to plunge into the open sea and swim straight down to the kind of dark, frigid depths where your imagination can be forgiven for getting away from

----

1 You can imagine the sort of thing:
  Man 1: 'The Doc says I stopped breathing for 22 seconds last night.'
  Man 2: 'That's it? Just 22 seconds? Hate to rain on your parade, sport, but two nights ago I went four minutes between breaths. They were measuring me up for a coffin when I snorted back to life. Never seen a worse case, they said.'
  Man 1: 'Your family must be very proud.'

you. When the surface appears as far away as a glinting star, 'What just brushed my leg?' is a question you may not want answered.

Freediving was contested at the 1900 Paris Olympics and competitors had to swim a maximum of 60 metres in the competition pool, with two points awarded for each metre swum and one point for each second they were submerged. It is a mostly individual sport in which a diver's main objective is to surpass either her own, or someone else's, established depth, distance or time. It takes place in swimming pools, lakes and open sea, and always begins with the diver in the water. Both a recreational and competition sport, freediving's various disciplines are differentiated by the type of assistance, if any, selected by the diver.

For instance, in the disciplines overseen by the Association Internationale pour le Développement de l'Apnée (the International Association for the Development of Apnoea, or AIDA), one of the sport's two governing bodies, a freediver has the following options—bearing in mind that in the depth disciplines a competition freediver must nominate the depth she hopes to achieve long before getting wet:[2]

- **Constant weight without fins:** Considered the purest and most difficult of the disciplines, the freediver must descend and ascend using only her own power. In addition to not wearing fins, a wetsuit and a weight belt, she must not pull on the weighted guide rope that links the surface craft to the base plate at the diver's chosen depth. On surfacing, a diver has 15 seconds to

---

2 The purpose of nominating a depth attempt is for safety and organizational reasons. Concerning the latter, a base plate needs to be set up at the nominated depth, and it's from this base plate that a diver retrieves a tag, which she needs to bring back to the surface with her. Having the base plate in place also takes emotion out of the equation, as divers who might choose to push past the base plate—thereby jeopardizing their safety—know the increased depth will not be considered official.

perform what is called a 'surface protocol'. This protocol, which must be performed after all dives, no matter what the discipline, involves removing the face mask, gesturing 'OK' with a hand, and giving a verbal 'I'm okay'.

- **Constant weight:** Though the diver is not permitted to touch the guide rope (other than to stop her descent), or change her ballast, she may wear fins.

- **Dynamic without fins:** Performed in a pool (minimum 25 metres), the freediver travels horizontally attempting to cover the greatest possible distance on a single breath. (Red-eyed children in backyard swimming pools unofficially perform such a discipline all the time.)

- **Dynamic with fins:** As above, except the freediver may wear fins or a mono-fin, which is a wide single fin accommodating both feet. It necessitates a dolphin-kick.

- **Static apnoea:** A freediver sits in a pool with her face submerged for as long as possible.[3]

- **Free Immersion:** No propulsion equipment (fins, weights, wet suits) is allowed, although the diver is permitted to pull on the rope during descent and ascent. Depending on the diver's preference this may be done feet first, head first, or alternating between the two.

- **Variable weight:** This allows a diver to use a weighted sled to drag herself under to the base plate. She may then use the guideline in her ascent.

- **No limits:** The diver may use any means to assist both her descent and ascent. Commonly, divers descend with a weighted sled and ascend with

---

3 Should you ever wish to attempt a personal record at static apnoea, ensure you are being monitored. Not only is it prudent to have help on hand in case of shallow-water blackout but, without a minder, you also run the risk of being 'rescued' by a passer-by just when you are on the verge of breaking your personal best.

the aid of an air-filled bag that is inflated when they've reached their chosen depth. Due to such assistance, no-limits divers descend to the greatest depths. In 2007, Austrian Herbert Nitsch reached a depth of 214 metres (see page 131 for other records).

It goes without saying that freediving, while potentially exhilarating, is certainly not the kind of thing your mother would ever be happy about you doing. Injuries to the inner ear caused by a failure to adequately equalize on descent are common. But it gets worse. Numerous people, including experienced freedivers, have died in the quest to push their bodies and their lungs to the limit.[4]

During dynamic and static apnoea, for instance, many fatalities are caused by shallow-water blackouts. A shallow-water blackout is when a diver loses consciousness underwater, even though they may not have necessarily experienced an urgent need to take another breath. The fainting is linked to latent hypoxia brought about by hyperventilation before a dive.

To be more specific, it is high levels of carbon dioxide (CO_2), rather than low levels of oxygen, that stimulate the need to breathe. But hyperventilation, which most divers practise before a dive, lowers the amount of CO_2 in the

----

4 According to a no-nonsense disclaimer on Freedive Australia's website (www.freedive.com.au):

'Freediving is a potentially dangerous activity and can lead to serious injury and death, even if all currently known limitations and safety guidelines are followed correctly. Accidents may be due to, but not limited to, drowning, shallow water blackout, defective gear, improper operation of boats, ear and sinus injuries, shark attack and others …

… EXTRA WARNING

Young adult males are the most likely to suffer from shallow water blackout—the most common freediving accident—and are expressly asked NOT TO BE DICKHEADS and to respect their own limitations. Always dive with a competent and alert buddy.

When you freedive, you assume all risks whether foreseen or unforeseen, of freediving.'

blood and effectively fools the body into believing it doesn't need to breathe even when oxygen stores are running dangerously low. When oxygen levels get low enough, a diver can lose consciousness—without seeing it coming—and drowning can result.

In depth diving, deep-water blackouts are common. These usually occur when a diver is in the last stages of ascent when there's a rapid drop in the partial pressure of oxygen in the lungs.

Such cases aside, that humans can survive so long without regular intakes of oxygen is due to both the body's natural way of adapting to trauma associated with a lack of oxygen, and the type of training free-divers do, which can involve holding your breath for a minute then going for a 400-metre stroll before taking another breath. In other words, nothing the majority of us would consider a fun time.

Under duress, our heart rate drops and our blood vessels shrink and blood is directed away from the limbs in order to benefit the more vital heart, brain and lungs. There is also another blood shift where blood plasma fills up blood vessels in the lungs and reduces residual volume. Without this adaptation, at depths greater than 30 metres the human lung would shrink and wrap into its walls, causing permanent damage.

AIDA-sanctioned freediving world records

Constant weight without fins

Women—Natalia Molchanova,
   Russia, 55 metres
Men—Martin Stepanek, Czech
   Republic, 83 metres

Constant weight

Women—Mandy-Rea Cruickshank,
   Canada, 88 metres
Men—Herbert Nitsch, Austria,
   111 metres

Dynamic without fins

Women—Natalia Molchanova,
   Russia, 149 metres
Men—Stig Aavall Severinsen,
   Denmark, 186 metres

Dynamic with fins

Women—Natalia Molchanova,
   Russia, 205 metres
Men—Stig Aavall Severinsen,
   Denmark, 225 metres

Static apnoea

Women—Natalia Molchanova,
   Russia, 8 minutes 0 seconds
Men—Tom Sietas, Germany,
   9 minutes 8 seconds

Free immersion

Women—Natalia Molchanova,
   Russia, 80 metres
Men—Martin Stepánek, Czech
   Republic, 106 metres

Variable weight

Women—Tanya Streeter, Cayman
   Islands, 122 metres
Men—Carlos Coste, Venezuela,
   140 metres

No limit

Women—Tanya Streeter, Cayman
   Islands, 160 metres
Men—Herbert Nitsch, Austria,
   214 metres

Hurling is an ancient Irish game that is similar to field hockey in that it is played outdoors on a rectangular field with a small ball and curved wooden sticks. More so than field hockey, however, it has overtones of combat. Thus the chances of getting belted across the side of the head are much higher in hurling than in hockey, not least because the ball can be played in the air and no law exists to prevent players from waving their sticks around like battle-axes in their attempts to whack it. Consequently, many hurling players who value their brains and their looks (rightly or wrongly) wear head and face protection.[1]

As in Gaelic football, another Irish game, the object of hurling is to score points by propelling the ball between an opponent's H-shaped goalposts, with

----

1 Some purists of the sport (that is, men with no teeth, battered noses and terrible short-term memories who played prior to the 1970s) may bemoan the relatively modern trend of wearing non-compulsory helmets and face protection. In *their* day you got smashed in the nose with a hurling stick and if you didn't like the way it felt you certainly didn't go around moaning about it. You just bled quietly, picked out any bone fragments floating about inside your nose and got on with the game … like a man.

more points being scored for a ball knocked under the crossbar (three points) than over it (one point).[2] This is because a goalkeeper—generally a fearless chap with no sense of self-preservation—protects the underside of the crossbar. In Gaelic football, a specialized ball similar to a football (soccer ball) is used and players are allowed to control it with their hands and feet. In hurling, a ball is usually propelled, on or off the ground, by a stick known as a hurley (or, in Irish, a *camán*).

A hurling ball (known as a sliotar or *sliothar*) is made of leather, has raised seams and measures about 24 centimetres in circumference. The game's signature piece, however, is the hurley, a stick made from ash (wood) generally 70–100 centimetres in length. It is distinctive for the curved, paddle-like surface (*bas*) at its end that is used to strike the ball—and how. A good clean hit can propel the ball distances close to 100 metres and at speeds nearing 150 kilometres per hour. For this reason, hurling is considered the fastest field-based ball-and-stick game in the world.

Hurling is played between two teams of fifteen men with the palest legs imaginable on a pitch approximately 137 metres long and 82 metres wide (it is the same pitch used for Gaelic football matches). Unlike field hockey, hurling

----

2 Umpires positioned near each goal have different ways of signalling scores. To signal a goal (under the crossbar), an umpire raises a green flag and places it to the left of the goal. To signal a point, he raises a white flag and places it to the right of goal.

More a ritual than a necessity, such flag waving is similar to what takes place in Australian Rules football, a game with similarities to Gaelic football except, among other things, it is played on an oval field with an oval ball. In 'Aussie Rules', as it's called, goal umpires also wave flags to signal either a goal (a ball kicked between two central parallel uprights) or a behind (a ball kicked either side of these uprights and within small posts set a few metres further out). Until recently, goal umpires inexplicably dressed in long white coats, like lab technicians, and took to all this flag waving with relish. Today, goal umpires still signal with flags, but they dress more sensibly.

players are allowed to handle the ball, although like most instances of ball handling in public, this must be done in moderation. A hurling player is not allowed to pick up a ball on the ground with his hands (so he dexterously flips it into his hands, even on the run, with his hurley), but he is permitted to catch a ball in flight, or knock it on to a team-mate. Once it is in his possession, however, he must take no more than four steps with the ball in hand. He is permitted, after those steps, to bounce the ball on the hurley and back into his hand and continue running another four steps. Since hurling players are forbidden to catch the ball more than twice in this way, they have become adept at running while balancing the ball on the end of the hurley. Hurley players would be shoo-ins at egg-and-spoon races.

As one might expect, hurling is a fast-paced, end-to-end sport that can be rather physical, particularly when the ball drops on the ground and a number of players rush towards it, hurleys raised, as if about to bludgeon a rat they've cornered in the kitchen. Shoulder charging or ice hockey-style bodychecks are not allowed but a measure of shoulder-to shoulder contact is permitted when two players are contesting the ball.

Most contact, however, is a by-product of tackling, which occurs when players attempt to stop each other hitting the ball by blocking the ball with their hurley, or hooking an opponent's hurley on its downswing. To a casual observer it may resemble a sword fight. With all this hurley-wielding going on, players do get struck with enthusiastically swung sticks, so it is not a game for the faint-hearted.

One of four Gaelic games,[3] it's believed hurling was brought to Ireland by the Celts some 2000 years ago, and it's a sport that echoes throughout Irish

----

3 The others are Gaelic football, rounders (a precursor to baseball) and handball (similar to squash, with a gloved hand used to hit the ball instead of a racquet).

folklore (the sport has a major role in the legend of Cú Chulainn, who was a Herculean type of folk hero[4]). In its earliest days hurling was played in many forms, often degenerating into violence. But in 1884, the Gaelic Athletic Association (which also oversees Gaelic football and a female version of hurling called camogie) was formed and a common set of written hurling rules was compiled. In 1887, the All-Ireland (Senior) Hurling Championships came into effect with counties Cork, Kilkenny and Tipperary by far the most successful to date.

Along with Gaelic football, hurling is the most popular sport in Ireland but it is also played in other countries where Irish expatriates are known to have settled. Which is pretty much everywhere.

---

4 Cú Chulainn was a name given to Sétanta, the nephew of King Conchobair mac Nessa of Ulster. Legend has it that one day Sétanta agreed to meet his uncle at a feast at the house of Culann as soon as he finished playing a hurling game. When Sétanta, whose skills with the hurley were unsurpassed, finally arrived at the house, he found it guarded by a fierce hound. The slavering beast was set to pounce on him when Sétanta used his hurley to drive a sliotar down the hound's throat. Sétanta then rushed the stunned beast, grabbed it by its feet and swung it around, smashing its head onto the flagstones, killing it. Thus Sétanta became known as Cú Chulainn, which translates as 'the hound of Culann'.

It's a grand legend, so it is, but it doesn't make clear whether or not Sétanta got his ball back.

Other stick-and-ball games

SHINTY

Said to derive from the same roots as hurling, shinty is a Scottish game
nowadays played almost exclusively in the Scottish Highlands. Like hurling, it
is played with a ball and a hooked stick on a rectangular pitch, but there are
numerous small differences: a shinty stick doesn't have the flat blade of a
hurley; shinty players are not allowed to handle the ball; a shinty goal is more
like a football (soccer) goal (thus the only score is one that goes past the
goalkeeper and into the goal); and the game is twelve-a-side. Shinty is one of
the forebears of ice hockey and bandy (see page 41). Informal ice or street
hockey games in Canada are still called shinny, after shinty.

LACROSSE

Invented by Native Americans,[5] lacrosse is a sport in which players use a stick
with a small pocket of netting at its end to propel a small hard rubber ball into

---

5 It's believed that in early forms of the game, rules were liberal by today's
standards. For one thing a stick was not only used for propelling the ball but for
walloping one's opponent. Such attacks—which were sometimes fatal—may
have given rise to the sporting cliché 'offence is the best form of defence'. Played
on fields miles long and wide, games could last for days. Early balls were made
out of many things, including wood, deerskin, clay, stone and even the heads of
the enemy. Basically, whatever came to hand.
    As a sport with a death toll might indicate, lacrosse, for the Native Americans,
was not undertaken lightly. It was a game of cultural and spiritual significance.

the opposition's goal. Played outdoors (on a rectangular pitch no larger than 100 metres by 54 metres) and indoors (on an ice rink that has been turfed over), it is as fast as hurling, while allowing considerably more contact. In fact, lacrosse (so named by early French explorers) shares many elements with ice hockey and bandy, as it permits front and side bodychecking (using your body to ram or shoulder charge someone with, or close to, the ball) and a degree of stick-to-body contact.

Played between two teams of ten players (or teams of six when played indoors), lacrosse allows team-mates to pass the ball between themselves and has no restrictions on how far a player can run with the ball in his crosse, or stick. However, there is a time restriction, which states that a team must shoot on goal within 30 seconds of securing the ball.

As with ice hockey, lacrosse goals are set in from each end line, meaning players can run around behind the goal and still be in the field of play.

An equestrian version of lacrosse is called polocrosse.

TOCCER

The name 'toccer' is an amalgamation of tennis and soccer, although the game more resembles hurling and lacrosse since players propel a ball into the opposition's goal, but using a tennis racquet instead of a stick. It appears to be the kind of thing a few kids devised on a long, hot and boring summer holiday when forced out from in front of the TV. As it happens this isn't far

----

from the truth, as it's believed that toccer was invented in 2002 by an American camp counsellor as a rainy-day cross-training game for tennis players.

Toccer (also known as tennis polo) is more of a casual, pick-up game, but rules set down by the Tennis Polo Association state that it is a seven-a-side game played on a field 75 yards by 55 yards with goals measuring 6 feet square—although soccer fields, and soccer goals, are often used despite both being larger. In play, tennis racquets are used to pass, carry, and pick up the ball. Incidental contact between players is allowed.

Considering the plethora of other stick-and-ball sports around the world, those waiting for toccer to be accepted into the Olympics should make sure they have a good book to read. It could take a while.

'Indian' horse racing

Every year, over four dimly lit August nights in the sagebrush country around Omak, Washington state, twenty horse riders race their steeds down a mountainside so precipitous it's known as 'Suicide Hill'. Almost more amazing than the willingness of riders to do such a thing in the near dark is that race organizers haven't tried to temper controversy by changing the name of the event, which has been known since the 1930s as the Omak Suicide Race. One would have thought that by now a spin-doctor would have been employed to re-badge the event as something more savoury.

In any case, the Omak Suicide Race is one of many so-called 'Indian' horse races that take place across the United States; races intended to showcase the bravery of riders (many of whom are Native American) and the willingness of horses to do as they're instructed, even if they think their riders are lunatics who just happen to be putting their equine lives at risk. In the case of the Omak Suicide Race, it is the highlight of an annual rodeo called the Omak

Stampede, with the main arena being the finishing post of the Suicide Race. The overall winner, dubbed the 'King of the Hill', is determined by how he placed in all four races.

The Suicide Race is modelled on races the local Native American tribes used to hold down nearby Keller Mountain (though never at night) and was established in 1935 as a draw-card event for the rodeo. The structure of the race has changed little since then, with the race beginning 50 feet from the bluff of Suicide Hill before riders plunge down the 50-degree slope for 225 feet, before sharply plunging into the Okanogan River, which is about as wide as a football field. Depending on the water level, horses will then gallop or swim across it before a final 500-foot gradual uphill sprint into the rodeo arena. It's all over in about a minute, albeit a dust-storming, whip-lashing, hell-raising one.

There can be little doubt that the Omak Suicide Race—which is still seen by some as a proving ground for young men of the Confederated Tribes of the Colville Reservation—calls for courage and expert horsemanship. It is, however, by far the most controversial of all Indian horse races, with animal welfare groups calling it one of the cruellest sporting events in the world—crueller for the fact it is held at night (each race is the show stopper to a night of rodeo action). Figures are imprecise but about twenty horses are believed to have died since 1983 (three died in 2004 alone). Some die of exhaustion, others are euthanazed on the spot after breaking a limb. Whether such horses could be said to have committed suicide is, in the circumstances, a moot point.

Supporters of the race acknowledge its risks but claim it is less dangerous than regular forms of horse racing and that all care is made to ensure that the twenty horses that qualify to contest the four races every year are at least five years old (to ensure fully developed bones), in excellent condition, good swimmers, not prone to baulking on hill tops and certainly not stoned or drunk. As the Suicide Race's Owners and Jockey's Association points out, 'changes in recent years ban alcohol and drugs for riders and animals'. And a good thing, too. Goodness knows how dangerous Suicide Hill would be to negotiate in the dark for a horse that's warmed up for the race with a joint and a bottle of bourbon.

Other distinctive horse races

THE PALIO DI SIENA

An occasion of much pageantry, puffy shirts and spectacularly silly hats, the *Palio di Siena* is an annual horse race around the cobblestones of the picturesque Piazza del Campo in the Italian city of Siena. A major tourist drawcard, the *Palio* is a race dating back more than 300 years between horses representing Siena's seventeen *contrade*, or wards. Two races are held every year on July 2 and August 16. As in *calcio storico Fiorentino* (see page 95), rivalries between *contrade* are fierce and barracking is enthusiastic, to say the least. Although both races are dedicated to the Virgin Mary, things have been known get a little unholy in the lead up to a race, and both horse and rider are guarded against any who may wish them ill.

Setting the *Palio di Siena* apart from most other horse races is the piazza setting (the Piazza del Campo is shaped like a medieval Roman amphitheatre)

----

and the almost reverential pageantry surrounding the event. During pre-race processions, trial races and the two official races, officials, horses and riders are resplendent in the traditional medieval costumes, colours and arms of each *contrade*[1]—ten of which are represented in each race (seven on merit, three drawn by lots). Add in tens of thousands of spectators—most of who are *contradaioli* (residents from rival contrades)—jammed in within and around the piazza, and the atmosphere fairly crackles.

The two races begin in the early evening—soon after a small explosive charge is set off within the piazza. If they are not spooked by the bang, the horses approach the starting line, which only has room for nine abreast. This leaves one horse, known as the *rincorsa*, staring at a lot of powerful backsides and cursing its luck. When all the horses are in correct position the starter, a local

----

----

1 The names, emblems and colours of each *contrade* are as follows: *Aquila* (Eagle), yellow with black and blue bands; *Bruco* (Caterpillar), yellow and green with blue bands; *Chiocciola* (Snail), yellow and red with blue bands; *Civetta* (Owl), black and red with white bands; *Drago* (Dragon), red and green with yellow bands; *Giraffa* (Giraffe), white and red; *Istrice* (Porcupine), white, red, black and blue bands; *Leocorno* (Unicorn), white and orange-yellow with blue bands; *Lupa* (She-Wolf), black and white with orange-yellow bands; *Nicchio* (Shell), blue with yellow and red bands; *Oca* (Goose), white and green with red bands; *Onda* (Wave), white and blue; *Pantera* (Panther), red and blue with white bands; *Selva* (Forest), green and orange with white bands; *Tartuca* (Tortoise), yellow and blue; *Torre* (Tower), dark Bordeaux red with white and blue bands; and *Valdimontone* (Ram), white and yellow with red bands.

authority called the *Mossiere*, instantly removes the *canape*, or the starting cord, and the race is on.

With the crowd's roar bristling their flanks, the horses must make three laps of the piazza, which is covered in dirt to allow the horses' hooves better purchase. Despite the dirt, a cobbled piazza is not designed for horse racing and it remains treacherous, as many animal rights activists have pointed out over the years—particularly since falls may lead to horses having to be put down. Adding to the objections of activists—not to mention to the general mayhem—is that riders are allowed to use whips … and not only on their own horses.

Fortunately, considering all the hazards, a rider does not necessarily have to be atop his bareback mount to win the race (which takes about 75 seconds). As long as his horse crosses the finish line in front, a winner it is. Somewhat cruelly, the loser is considered to be the *contrada* whose horse came second.

Winning the *Palio di Siena* affords bragging rights to *contradaioli* who, after collecting their winnings and rubbing their rivals' faces in it (spot fires of violence are known to break out following a race), presumably repair to the nearest drinking hole to celebrate, so long and so hard that the next morning's sun will beat them home. Winning the Palio also earns the victorious *contrada* a trophy—a banner of painted silk, or *palio*, which is created anew for every race.

THE TOM QUILTY GOLD CUP

Widely regarded as Australia's most punishing long-distance horse race
(and one of the most prestigious races of its kind in the world), the Tom Quilty
Gold Cup is a one-day race of 160 kilometres through varying and challenging
terrains and weather conditions. At its foundations is the belief of creator
R M Williams, and of inaugural sponsor Tom Quilty (a famous Australian
horseman), that a good horse could be ridden 100 miles in a day to post a
letter and still be fit for work the next day. Considering such demands, horses
must be as grateful as anyone for the invention of email, thus preventing them
from slogging it out just so their owner could send his great-aunt a poorly
spelt missive wholly concerned with the lack of rain and his fruitless search
for a good woman—*any* woman, in fact.

The invention of email notwithstanding, this endurance race has been held
annually since 1966. The race starts at midnight and takes place in a different
location each year, one selected for the breadth of its terrain. Each rider
attempts to finish the race within 24 hours, and to do so their horses must
be passed fit by veterinarians after each 35-kilometre stage.

Kabaddi

Particularly popular on the Asian subcontinent, kabaddi is surely the only sport besides synchronized swimming in which participants not only hold hands with their team-mates but also hold their breath. The punch line, of course, is that kabaddi is played on land where air isn't usually an issue.

Kabaddi is a seven-a-side, points-scoring game that requires no equipment (which explains its popularity in rural areas) and, for male competitors at least, very little clothing. Unlike in beach volleyball—another sport that requires, if not demands, brief attire—a kabaddi competitor's exposed flesh is more a tactical device than a marketing one. This is because his state of near undress arguably gives his grappling opponents less to grab hold of during play. Which, of course, explains why shorts, unlike shirts, are *always* worn.[1]

---

1 Kabaddi players in the past often wore as little as a pair of underpants and, for a reason no one could ever sufficiently explain, their socks. As such, games of kabaddi often resembled a disagreement in a men's changing room.

In kabaddi, teams take turns sending a lone raider into the opposition's half of the court—a flat 12.5 metre by 10 metre area covered in dirt, grass, or, when played indoors, synthetic floor tiles. The raider's objective is to tag (touch) as many members of the opposing team (called anti-raiders, or 'antis') as possible before returning at haste to his team's half of the court. During a raid, the antis, who must stay within the boundaries of their half or be given 'out', form a human chain which they do by either holding each other's arms or holding hands.

Complicating matters for the raider is that he must conduct his daring raid and return to his own half on a single breath of air. Why? Because it is in the rules. And to ensure he doesn't just puff out his cheeks and sneak breaths through his nose (as surely happened when the game was played, unsuccessfully one supposes, for the first time), a raider must loudly and clearly chant 'kabaddi' over and over again until he crosses back over the centre line.[2] Should his cant, as it's called, ever cease, pause, or change, he will be given out. With such an unusual rule of play one might assume the sport's exponents have their work cut out for them in pushing for kabaddi to become a fully-fledged Olympic event.[3]

If maintaining the cant isn't challenging enough—to both a raider's lung power and his sense of the absurd—he must also evade being captured. Should a raider manage to tag an anti and return to his half on a single breath of air, he scores a point for his team and the anti he tagged is eliminated from the game (temporarily or permanently, depending on the version of kabaddi

---

2 The word kabaddi is translated from the Hindi for 'holding of breath' and not, as some may think, 'you're kidding me'.

3 Kabaddi was a demonstration sport at the 1936 Olympics in Berlin, and it was included for the first time in the Asian Games held in Beijing in 1990. There are various kabaddi associations and competitions throughout the world.

played). However, should an anti manage to physically restrain the raider and prevent him from touching his home ground with any part of his body before his breath runs out (and his cant consequently, and mercifully, stops), the anti-raiders score a point and the raider is out and must leave the field. As such, kabaddi has elements of wrestling, which—possibly along with rich kormas and lard-based dhals—could explain the robust size of elite competitors.

The origins of kabaddi are difficult to pinpoint but the popular belief is that the game originated about 4000 years ago in either of the Indian states of Punjab or Tamil Nadu. Some argue that it was devised as a way to develop physical strength and speed in young men. The Southampton Kabaddi Association (kabaddi.co.uk) takes such a position and runs with it, suggesting kabaddi is even more effective than juvenile detention in controlling rampant youth.[4]

Since then, the game has spread around Asia and the world, and is known by various names depending on the cant. Thus, the game and the cant are *teechub* in Indonesia, *chedigudu* in Malaysia, *gudu* in Sri Lanka and *do-do* in Nepal.

---

4 'Indirectly, Kabaddi can have an impact by providing challenge and adventure, and by giving meaning and a sense of purpose to young people's lives where previously there was a vacuum. Kabaddi delivered in a sound ethical framework can engender self-respect, self-esteem, confidence and leadership abilities.'

Another breath-holding sport

SYNCHRONIZED SWIMMING

Much to the bemusement—if not consternation—of many, synchronized swimming has been an official Olympic sport since 1984, despite the fact competitors compete in make-up, wear clips on their noses and often enter the water like falling dominoes, as if acting in a cheesy 1940s Esther Williams 'aqua-musical'. An aquatic version of dance, synchronized swimming (at Olympic level) sees women in teams of two or eight perform—to the kind of teeth-grinding music you tend to hear in elevators—stylistic routines while upright, horizontal or inverted, in a deep body of water. Marks are awarded for both performance and artistic impression.

Despite the scorn the sport regularly attracts, Olympic-level synchronized swimmers are highly trained elite athletes who have the lung power, strength and presence of mind to perform complex, synchronized routines with a partner or partners while in the water. And they make it look so effortless. If they are not holding themselves up out of the drink at waist level—while semaphoring their arms frantically, as if warning approaching tankers of rocks ahead—they are doing the same thing with their legs while upside down in the water. Critics may grudgingly accept that synchronized swimmers are finely prepared, highly athletic performers who have strong legs and lungs the size of Liechtenstein, but they question whether synchronized swimming meets the criteria of a sport and, even if it does, whether it belongs at the Olympic Games, the supposed pinnacle of world sport.

Synchronized swimming as an organized sport first started in the 1890s, when it was first performed by men—a chilling thought, arguably, when you picture men in brief swimming attire scissoring their legs out of the water. The direction of the sport changed in 1907, however, when Australian Annette Kellerman performed ballet-like routines in a glass tank of water at the New York Hippodrome. Esther Williams, Hollywood star and former US freestyle champion, headlined in a cinematic remake of Kellerman's life called *Million Dollar Mermaid*.

Williams' follow up aqua-musicals saw synchronized swimming surge in popularity and it became a demonstration sport at the 1960 Rome Olympics.

For other breath-holding sports, see Freediving (page 126) and Underwater Hockey (page 241).

Korfball

Sometimes ridiculed by men in order to emphasize their supposedly irreproachable masculinity, korfball is a non-contact, mixed-gender sport that most resembles netball. With its philosophy of fair play—and the subjugation of individual strength and skill in favour of team cohesion—fans of the game might choose to describe it as the complete sport. Critics of the sport, however, like the aforementioned men, might deem it a game for sissies. The fact that korfball's scoring targets are cane baskets—similar to those found on the front of a girl's bicycle—only encourages them.

Played indoors or outdoors, korfball is contested by two teams of eight players (four men and four women) on a tennis-court-sized playing area, which is divided into two halves called zones. The object of the game is to throw the ball through the baskets placed atop 3.5-metre-high poles found in each zone. Unlike in netball or basketball, where the target rings are found midway along their respective court's back line, korfball's two baskets are found about two thirds the way into each zone, enabling shots on goal from 360 degrees.

Perhaps the standout feature of korfball is its strict philosophy of team over individuals. One rule that bears this out more than any other is the one that forbids players to run with the ball—thus preventing any particularly gifted individuals from slaloming through the opposition and winning a game single-handedly. So, like netball, korfball is one of the few sports in the world in which, when you receive the ball, you have only one step in which to stop. Consequently, the ball is moved around the court through swift passing to players who position themselves in open space.

In addition to the above rule, korfball is strictly non-contact. Not only is any form of tackling, holding or blocking forbidden but players cannot even shoot for goal if a defender has taken up position in front of them. In such a case, an attacker must look to pass the ball. Such rules are designed to negate the advantage of height and put males and females on a similar footing.

Dutch schoolteacher Nico Broekhuysen invented korfball in the early twentieth century. Broekhuysen adapted the game from a Swedish sport called ringboll. Broekhuysen replaced ringboll's ring with a basket (*korf* is Dutch for basket) and he also introduced many rules to allow his school's male and female students to play together. For example, all marking contests must be one on one and players may only mark someone of the same sex.

Due to its origins, korfball is most popular in the Netherlands, although dozens of countries have korfball associations and competitions. There is an annual world championship and korfball has twice been an Olympic demonstration sport—in Antwerp in 1920 and Amsterdam in 1928.

Other sports with mixed-gender teams

NETBALL

Netball is most popular in Commonwealth countries such as England, Australia, New Zealand and Jamaica. Girls and women usually play netball but men are increasingly playing the game, in male only and mixed teams. Of the seven on-court players in a mixed netball team, no more than three may be men. Unlike korfball, there are no marking restrictions, meaning men can defend women and vice versa. Mixed netball teams are often made up of people from the same workplace. And since, traditionally, few of the men have played before, they have a poor grasp of netball's very particular and idiosyncratic rules, and tend to lack finesse. Thus they sometimes approach the game as a bull approaches a spot of shopping in a china shop.

TENNIS

Mixed doubles has been a tennis discipline since Pimms was found to go very nicely with lemonade. Still played at grand slam level, mixed doubles usually features specialist doubles players because star singles players rarely find the time or inclination to play. There are no differences between the rules for doubles and mixed doubles, meaning male and female players may serve to, and rally with, each other.

SUB FOOTBALL

Created and played in Auckland, New Zealand, and also played in Melbourne, Australia, Sub Football is a shortened version of football (soccer). In Sub Football, however, points are awarded not only for scoring a goal but also for narrowly missing, which seems exceedingly generous. Played on a field approximately 60 metres by 40 metres, Sub Football's two goals are flanked on both sides by 60-centimetre-high, 2-metre-wide boards which, if hit by a ball, count as one point to the attacking side. A regulation goal counts as three points. With a maximum of three (out of six) outfield players allowed to be male, Sub Football shares a similar philosophical outlook to korfball since, unlike full-field soccer or indoor soccer, contact is all but disallowed. Such a rule is intended to limit the benefits of strength and make the game more attractive to women.

LAND diving

Usually when the agriculturally minded want to celebrate a harvest and plan for the next they wipe the sweat from their brows, enjoy a few drinks, oil the plough and perhaps even direct a prayer or two to whichever god is in charge of the weather. On the tiny Vanuatuan island of Pentecost, however, they strip naked, cover their modesty with a sheath (long and pointy enough to take out an eye) and throw themselves off a rickety, 25-metre tower with only tree vines tied around their ankles to break their fall and prevent possible death.

Land diving, or *naghol*, has been practised at Pentecost Island's southern villages for as long as anyone there can remember. While it has become a ceremonial way to ensure a good yam harvest, the practice actually has its roots in domestic violence, a sad fact that surely makes it unique in the world of sport. Legend has it that a woman climbed a banyan tree in order to escape her abusive husband. The irate husband, who unsurprisingly failed to coax her down with the promise of a shorter beating, climbed up after her. When the woman jumped from the top branches he jumped after her, not realizing she had tied a vine around her ankles. In a flash her domestic violence problems were solved.

For some time, perhaps as an act of ceremonial solidarity, it was only women who performed land diving. Today, however, only men and boys[1] take the risky plunge, after elders decided it was something only males should do in order to redress their legacy of shame—something about the sins of the fathers being visited upon the sons. How the island's young men feel about this isn't known but it seems safe to assume that in the lead-up to the ceremony they spend more than a little time wishing they'd been born girls.

Land diving takes place every year in April, May and June. Just prior to the opening of land diving season, Pentecost Island's menfolk erect the land-diving tower—which resembles builder's scaffolding in countries with a lax attitude to workplace safety—laying platforms at various heights. Made from freshly cut wood (the fresher it is, the stronger it is) and lashed together with vines, it is erected on the side of a hill. It affords magnificent views of the rugged coastline, presumably as a concession to jumpers. If you're going to end up dead or maimed as a result of a jump gone wrong, best that the last thing you see (besides the ground looming up at you, of course) is easy on the eye.

Once the 20–30-metre tower is built, the process of selecting suitable vines for the *naghol* begins. Such vines need to be supple and elastic with plenty of sap inside to ensure they don't simply snap when under extension. When the vines are selected the ends are shredded, so that they can be secured to the top of the tower and, eventually, to the diver's ankles (different vines are used

---

1 That parents allow their young sons to perform the death-inviting dive certainly puts into perspective the Western trend to wrap children in cotton wool lest life encroach upon them and threaten their delicate equilibrium.

depending on the weight of the diver). Good judgment in the selection of vines is crucial since miscalculation can see the vine snap, sending the diver slamming into the sloping ground (which does allow for some margin for error, unlike, say, a horizontal slab of concrete). As some jumpers leap from as high as 30 metres, such a fall can prove fatal.

Typically, when a jumper has climbed the scaffolding and has his vine secured he wonders how he got roped into all this and thinks of all the things he may never get to do. Below him the women of Pentecost Island perform a loud ceremonial dance. They are bare-chested, further reminding the diver what he has to lose if things go awry. When the women have completed their dance the diver claps, psyches himself up then spreads his arms out. Then he jumps, head first, towards the ground.

Unlike bungee jumpers (see opposite), land divers do not bounce all over the place after a jump. Vines are not that elastic. In fact, it's normal, even desirable, for divers to make some contact with the ground, since it's believed a diver's hair brushing the soil during a jump will add to the soil's fertility. Sometimes more than a diver's hair makes contact with the earth. It's said that in 1974, when Queen Elizabeth II visited Vanuatu, she watched the Pentecost islanders do their thing. Unfortunately it wasn't a good season for vines. They were so dry that many divers hit the ground after their vines snapped. One later died.

Today, land diving is a significant tourist attraction. The villagers earn money from tour companies who ship out foreigners in khaki shorts and loud shirts to marvel at the islanders' exploits. Quite obviously, the islanders earn every penny.

Another sport where you take a plunge

Compared to land diving, bungee (or bungy) jumping seems almost cowardly. Then again, if you were standing atop a 100-metre chasm with only a long ribbon of elastic preventing certain death you probably wouldn't countenance such a view. You'd be too busy quivering in abject fear.

Inspired by land diving, the first known bungee jump took place on 1 April 1979 (fittingly, April Fool's Day). Four members of an Oxford University group calling themselves The Dangerous Sports Club leapt from the 245-foot Clifton Suspension Bridge in Bristol, England. Delighted to survive the jump (though it did lead to their arrest), they began to jump from other structures of frightening heights, such as the Golden Gate Bridge in San Francisco.

In the mid 1980s, New Zealander A J Hackett (who, in the spirit of adventure and commercial enterprise, has jumped from a number of well-known landmarks, such as the Eiffel Tower) turned bungee jumping into a commercial concern and today it is practised in numerous countries—though most often from tall cranes and purpose-built platforms, as authorities don't tend to look too favourably on people using landmarks as equipment in extreme sport.

Bungee cords tend to be made from pre-stressed latex cord, which is braided into a thick rope. As with picking the right vine for land diving, a bungee cord must cater to the jumper. If the bungee cord is too short, the jump loses some

----

of its thrill (if, indeed, getting close to hitting the ground is a thrill). If it's too long, the bungee operator will have to explain herself to the police and the deceased's family. Of course, it should be remembered that the length of a bungee cord is measured when it is stretched to its limit.

Nowadays bungee jumping has a few spin-off activities. Variations include the catapult, where the subject begins on the ground and is shot into the air, and the bungee swing, where a free fall segues into a long speedy swing as the bungee cord is attached to a point far away from the jump location.

To take part in Turkey's national sport, *yagli güres*, a man needs to strip down to a pair of hand-stitched, shin-length leather pants and smother himself in olive oil from head to toe. Although this kind of activity usually takes place in shady venues pejoratively described as 'dens', oil wrestling is watched and beloved by Turks of all ages who, though willing to embrace their European heritage, are, rightly, not willing to let go of their Asian traditions—even if they do seem wildly homoerotic.[1]

The spiritual home of oil wrestling—a sport that stretches back half a millennium to the days of the Ottomans (as in Empire, not footstools)—is

---

1 It is, admittedly, a cliché to point out the homoerotic overtones of oil wrestling, what with the leather pants, oil-smearing and grappling. But what with the leather pants, oil-smearing and grappling, there seems no other option. This isn't to say, of course, that one would confront a Turkish wrestler in person and tease him about his sport. Well, not unless you knew for sure you could outrun him.

Edirne, a large town near Turkey's border with Greece. Turkey's biggest oil-wrestling tournament—the Kirkpinar festival—takes place every June at the purpose-built Sarayiçi stadium. It attracts hundreds of *pehlivan* (wrestlers) from all over the country, most of whom compete in the free weight category. But oil wrestling is held all over the country at different times of the year and the rituals are more or less the same.

The pre-tournament routine begins with competitors thoroughly oiling themselves and any fellow competitors who may be having trouble reaching a few hard-to-get places. As you might expect, the oil makes it exceedingly difficult for wrestlers to get a grip on each other, which is why it is common for wrestlers to grab each other by the belt that holds up their pants (known as *kispet*). They may even thrust a hand *inside* their opponent's *kispet*, in their attempts to bring him to the ground. Just when and why the oil was introduced isn't known, but it's safe to say the person who came up with the idea either wanted the bouts to last a long time or had a predilection for seeing strong men slicked up like otters.

Even though the wrestling is the centre of a festival, much goes on around the arena while the wrestlers prepare, not least a lot of picnicking by fans. Meanwhile, inside the arena (the surface of which is covered in lush grass), the beat of drums is as common as the voice of the ground announcer, the *cazgir*, who, figuratively speaking, wears many hats. Not only does he keep fans abreast of the competition and lavish competitors with sometimes politically incorrect praise ('Every woman can give birth; but not every boy can be a wrestler,' has been heard from at least one *cazgir*), but he also leads prayers[2] and recites what he feels is appropriate poetry.

---

2 Prayers such as: '*Allah, Allah, Illallah / May we prosper / Our patron is Hamza the wrestler / Our ancestors were wrestlers / Two valiant men take the field / One is blond, one dark / Both are keen to win the prize / Do not despair when down /*

One of his first roles, however, is to introduce the *kurban*, the ritual slaughtering of an animal in the Halal way with prayers offered to Allah. The blood of the animal (usually a goat) having been spilt, the tournament is almost ready to commence, starting with the youngest competitors and working up to the elite; powerful men built not so much like body builders, with their fussed over, look-at-me muscle definition, but more like bulls— slabs of meat knotted together with muscles the size of bread loaves.

When they are ready to begin, the *cazgir* introduces each *pehlivan* to the crowd then launches into a prayer, during which the wrestlers stand in a line facing Mecca before kneeling on the ground and saying to themselves:

> **Wrestler, don't feel pride at your strength, intelligence, wealth and position. You came from the soil and you will return to the soil. You were absent and you will be absent. You will account for the power that you have in the next world, to Allah. Use your power for right and justice, to prevent oppression and not to torment.**

After the wonderful prayer has been offered, the *pehlivan* form lines and skip across the field, about half a dozen at a time, slapping their knees and jumping as they move forward. Then they face their opponents and, with referees on hand, begin their bouts. Numerous match-ups (which, in terms of technique, resemble Greco-Roman wrestling) take place simultaneously.

For three days *pehlivan* compete in elimination bouts, which, due largely to the oil, can last for a maximum of 40 minutes (20 minutes for juniors). If at the

----

Do not boast when up / When above, do not loosen your grip / Meet leg trip with leg trip / Offer a prayer to Mohammed / I hastened to the spring / May Allah be with you both.'

40-minute mark one of the contestants hasn't had his shoulders pinned to the ground, or been lifted off his feet with his attacker taking three steps, judges will award the bout on points accrued.

It's always a harsh way to lose a bout but infinitely better than when the sport was first played. With no bouts awarded on a points basis, someone had to be pinned (no matter how long it took) or killed in order for the contest to end.

Other traditional Turkish sports

CAMEL FIGHTING

It has been said that camel fighting is to Turks what bullfighting is to Spaniards, but such a comparison suggests camel fighting is a duel between human and beast. It isn't. Camel fighting pits camel against camel.

A legacy from ancient tribes—and still enjoyed by nomads, particularly in the Aegean region—camel fighting is a winter sport because winter is the camel's mating season. It seems that when winter falls and a male camel's eye starts a' rovin', he is instinctively ready to knock down a rival should any long-legged, long-lashed female saunter into the picture. Very primitive, but in the camels' defence, nothing you don't see at a nightclub every Saturday night.

A fight begins when two camels (which can weigh as much as a tonne each) are brought into proximity and a female camel (a cow) is paraded around them

---

in order to drive them into a lather. Sometimes one turns tail before so much as an insult has been traded, and that camel effectively forfeits the match and, presumably, gets a bad write-up in the press the next day. More often, however, much to the excitement of the ground announcer, the two camels rush at each other and crash shoulders, beginning what looks like a wrestling match. The barging and spit flying can go on for some time until one camel is knocked, or tripped, to the ground and is thus defeated.

Camels are muzzled, so injuries are rare, which isn't to say animal welfare groups would look on the sport too favourably; though it seems rather harmless when compared to dog fighting and cock fighting.

If winning a camel-fighting tournament brings kudos to a camel (which is pampered by its owner and rested for nine months of the year), it also rewards the owner, who not only becomes a celebrity in his village but also the proud owner of a new carpet.

CIRIT

Cirit (pronounced jir-IT) is as much a ceremony as a sports event and has been played by Turks for centuries. Today, playing *cirit* is not as widespread as it once was and is often just reserved for weddings and holidays.[3] Ordinarily a fun game at a wedding might seem just the ticket, but when it becomes

---

3 The tradition of *cirit* is still alive in Iran, Afghanistan, Turkmenistan and other Asian countries inhabited by people of Turkish origin.

apparent that injuries and even death can occur from playing *cirit*, you might wonder at the wisdom of such event-scheduling. You can't help but think a violent death might be a bit of a downer during your average wedding.

That said, according to the Republic of Turkey Ministry of Culture and Tourism (www.kulturturizm.gov.tr), 'a player who dies in the course of a game is considered to have perished in battle, so his surviving relatives don't seek redress against the other player. Fathers even boast about their sons who lost their lives while taking part in the game.'

As this suggests, *cirit* is a highly respected sport that references the skills and bravery of men and horses in battle.[4] Two teams of seven players play the game on a field measuring 70–120 metres long. Forming rows within their respective safety zones, the two teams (who are mounted on horses and wearing regional costumes) face each other from across the field. In each player's right hand is a 70–110-centimetre-long, javelin-like piece of wood called a *cirit*. In his left hand are extra *cirits*. While *cirits* are now light and blunted at each end, with rubber tips, there was a time when they were heavier and pointier and capable of even more damage.

---

4 Turks brought this horse-riding game with them in their journey from Central Asia to Anatolia. Ottoman cavalrymen used it to maintain the fitness of their horses and soldiers. For Turks, the horse was both sacred and indispensable and at one time they spent every day of their life in the company of horses. Horses were their workmates, friends and even sources of nourishment, with *kumiss* (mare's milk) being their staple drink.

At the commencement of the game a player from one team (let's call him Player A) rides forward until he is within about 10 metres of the other team. After much jockeying, during which he's careful not to enter the opposition's safety zone, Player A hurls his *cirit* at any one of the opposition players, who will either attempt to dodge the missile or, more spectacularly, catch it. A catch would earn this player (let's call him Player B) three points, although if he's hit by the *cirit*, Player A's team is awarded six points.

It's at this stage the game heats up, for as soon as Player A has thrown his *cirit* he turns his horse and high-tails it back to his safety zone, as fast as he can, because he knows Player B will be in pursuit and attempting to hit him with a *cirit* or two of his own. Again, if Player B hits Player A he will score six points, or if Player A catches the *cirit* thrown at him he will earn three points. (Points are also awarded for spectacular evasive manoeuvres, while points are deducted for falling off a horse or riding out of bounds.) Once Player A has reached his safety zone he cannot be hit and that skirmish is over. Another player from Player A's team then rides out to the opposition to begin another skirmish.

When all competitors from Player A's side have initiated a skirmish, the first round is over. The second and final round then commences with competitors from Player B's team initiating each skirmish.

One intriguing rule, of which Turks are rightly proud, awards points to a player who shows mercy towards an opponent. Should a pursuing *cirit* player draw level with his retreating opponent, he can choose not to throw his *cirit* from

----

----

point blank range but, rather, announce that he is sparing him. This show of sportsmanship awards the merciful player three points and spares his opponent a possible whack in the back of the head—what's known as a win-win situation.

Some see it as an extreme sport, others as a discipline, an art, even a philosophy. In any case, parkour is just the kind of thing that would come in handy if you were confronted on an urban high street by an army recruiter, or a burly man with acute anger management issues and an axe to grind.

Sometimes called 'obstacle coursing', parkour (from the French *parcours*, which means 'route') is the means of making one's way through any kind of environment as quickly, efficiently and directly as possible, using an array of almost balletic jumps, vaults, leaps, climbs and rolls. When performed by the most highly practised *traceurs* (as male parkour practitioners are sometimes known; a female is a *traceuse*), parkour can almost defy belief, not to mention good sense. Though most parkour is performed close to ground level, very occasionally it takes to the skies where it seems the most direct route between one rooftop and another is not via two sets of lifts or stairways but by a well-executed leap and roll that would make Batman proud. Miscalculations can be—and have been—fatal.

Though human beings have been practising parkour-like movements ever since large carnivores first got a whiff of us, parkour, as a discipline, originated in the Parisian suburb of Lisses in the late 1980s when founder David Belle[1]—inspired by military obstacle courses and comic-book heroes—began exploring the notion of escape and pursuit for their own sake. Thus, in imagining racing from point A to point B through the urban streetscape, Belle would look to take as direct a route as possible by adapting his body, as fluidly as he could, to whatever obstacles he came upon—be it a wall, a railing, a set of stairs, whatever. With close friend Sébastien Foucan, he developed parkour, a virtual art of movement with a number of specific moves.[2]

A committed *traceur* spends considerable time honing his skills despite the fairly slim chance of ever having to execute them in a real-life situation—which just emphasizes that the real point of parkour is in the expression and joy of movement. While some are able to practise at specialized gyms made soft with matting, most *traceurs* practise in the city, using human-made obstacles in much the same way as skateboarders. However, unlike skateboarders, who have a slouchy, rebellious cool about them, *traceurs* are more likely to be the quiet types who foster a love of computer games, superheroes and imaginary planets called Zorgon.[3] That parkour gets them out of the house and exercising can only be a good thing.

----

1 Belle has starred in a number of films (such as the 2004 French action film *Banlieue 13*) and TV commercials (such as the BBC's 'Rush Hour') practising parkour. Parkour has also featured prominently in many other films, from 2006's *Casino Royale* to almost everything Jackie Chan has ever made.

2 These include: Tic Tac—jumping towards a wall, leading with a foot, and using the wall as a kind of springboard from which to jump either higher or in a different direction; and The Kong—a vault used to traverse a chest high wall where the *traceur* dives towards the wall, places both hands flat on its top then brings his knees through his arms in one smooth motion.

3 This is a wild and unsubstantiated generalization.

Like most extreme sports, parkour attracts its share of controversy, not least from those whose knowledge of it is based solely on TV clips of *traceurs* jumping from one rooftop to another 10 metres below. The sport certainly has its dangers (rarely to life, more frequently to limb) but organized groups of *traceurs* who follow the broad philosophy preached by Belle stress that enthusiasts practise in groups and stick to moves commensurate with their level of skill. They also point out that parkour is about discipline and self-improvement, not competition. In recent times, however, small competitions have started to emerge. Whether these are followed by larger, organized competitive events—as happens with trick skateboarding—only time will tell.

Among *traceurs* there is also considerable controversy about what is or isn't parkour. Fundamentalists eschew any kind of embellishment or trick in the course of motion, such as a back flip, which serves no practical purpose. They rightly argue that if you were fleeing somebody, you would not waste time showing your pursuer your Nadia Comaneci impression. Due to this controversy, a schism has emerged in the parkour world and the parallel strain—developed by Foucan[4]—is known as 'free running'. Practitioners of free running believe tricks add to the fun and the self-expression. As they reason, why not add a somersault when you jump off a window ledge to the street below?

An interesting question, the rest of us think, as we take the stairs.

----

4 In a 2003 interview Sebastien Foucan described walking as a 'wasted opportunity'. A more imaginative approach to walking, he said, would turn a rock, a tree and a lamppost into, respectively, a launch pad, a swing and a ladder. 'Ideally, the street would be covered with [such] obstacles.'

Pillow Fighting

It is, admittedly, a stretch to consider pillow fighting anything but an amusing—though sometimes headache-inducing—game played mostly by children.[1] Lacking any formality, a pillow fight involves two or more people battering each other around the head and body with plump pillows until one gives up or exhaustion takes its toll. It can be a surprisingly satisfying pursuit.

Pillow fights can be scheduled affairs (such as, 'Pillow fight, my room, ten minutes') but quite often they are impromptu, beginning with a king hit; someone walking into her bedroom, and minding her own business, is startled by a pillow swung into her face with as much force as the assailant can

---

1 Teenagers of both sexes also enjoy the pursuit although, contrary to the wishful thinking of some (many of whom are old enough to know better), young women enjoying slumber parties don't tend to strip down to their scanties before getting out the Tontines and giving each other a jolly good pillowing.

muster. The victim grabs a pillow of her own and a battle then ensues with the chance of any real injury negligible, notwithstanding dodging a cushioned blow, losing balance and falling onto a side table or, who knows, a nest of scorpions carelessly left lying on the ground.

While most people are content for pillow fighting to remain a niche household game, some have attempted to elevate it into regulated competition, not least the organizers of the so-called World Pillow Fighting Championships which, although the 2007 event was cancelled, have been held every Independence Day (July 4) in Kenwood, California, since the mid 1960s.

Open to anyone over the age of fourteen (which unfortunately precludes many ardent students of the art), the championships begin with all competitors placed in a draw, after which a series of knockout matches is held. Each bout takes place on a slippery pole that is suspended over a mud pit. Before fighting begins, combatants straddle the pole and shimmy into position, facing each other.

On the commencement of the contest, pillow fighters are not allowed to touch the pole with their hands or use their feet to dislodge their opponent. The competitors' wet feather pillows can be held in either or both hands but must be swung at least every 30 seconds. If a minute passes without anyone falling into the mud the bout continues with both competitors having to place one hand behind their backs. The first competitor to knock her opponent into the mud wins the fall. Two out of three falls wins the bout.

Like the World Pillow Fighting Championships, the Toronto-based Pillow Fight League (PFL) has made efforts to take pillow fighting from the bedrooms of the world out into the public arena. Represented by its cadre of more than twenty female pillow fighters, the PFL (their slogan is 'Fight like a girl') has borrowed heavily from burlesque, vaudeville, professional wrestling and old travelling boxing troupes and, depending on who you ask, the result is either a return to the worst days of sexism or a spectacle that is empowering to women in an ironic, post-modern way.

Since 2004, pillow fighters with nom de plumes such as Betty Clocker, Sarah Bellum and Polly Esther have been battling it out—and hamming it up with trash talk—on padded mats in front of crowds of young professionals, in Canadian and US nightclubs.[2] Best of all, for the women in the audience who dream of socking another woman with a juicy pillow in front of an enthusiastic audience, the PFL sometimes hosts try-outs. Pillow fighting could not only be a hobby, but a paid job. Enlightened times.

---

2 According to the PFL's website, www.gopfl.com, combat rules are as follows:
  '1. Female pillow fighters only. No exceptions.
  2. Professional pillow fights are won via pinfall, surrender, or referee stoppage. If a pillow fight ends at the time limit with no winner, a winner is declared by a three-judge committee, using the traditional 10 point system. Pillow fighters are judged based on Style, Stamina, and the Eye of the Tiger.
  3. Pillow fighting is Fun. No biting, scratching or hair pulling. Malicious intent and blatant disregard of your opponent's safety (or your own) may result in immediate suspension and/or dismissal from the League.
  4. Mouth guards, kneepads and elbow pads are mandatory.
  5. Bearing in mind Rule #3, most anything goes in a pillow fight, as long as there is a pillow at the point of contact. Preventing your opponent's offence by holding her pillow is not allowed.
  6. Pillow fighters must practise good sportswomanship. No rude, lewd or suggestive behavior.
  7. A pillow is not a weapon. Deliberately compressing the pillow fibres to increase the density of the pillow is not allowed. Loading a pillow with a foreign object is strictly forbidden.'

RACE walking

Race walking may be an established Olympic and world championship sport contested by athletes from numerous countries, but to the average outsider it remains the most unfathomable of athletic activities. To many, a competition for walking as quickly as one can (without ever running) makes about as much sense as a competition for running as slowly as one can (without ever walking). It all makes more sense than your average David Lynch film, however, but that, admittedly, is irrelevant.

That aside, race walking is a challenging sport, not only because the standard Olympic race walking distances are 20 kilometres for women, and 20 kilometres and 50 kilometres for men. But the biomechanics of walking quickly without breaking into a run means that race walkers' bodies contort so much that at full pelt they resemble the cartoonishly camp Mr Humphries, from *Are You Being Served*[1], mincing over a bed of hot coals—the hips sway

---

1 Young readers should count themselves fortunate they've never heard of, let alone seen, this 1970s British sitcom, which is set in a department store. Suffice

violently, the shoulders sashay, the arms pump and the legs make countless little steps.

There's no doubt that race walkers are fine athletes who do their utmost within the restrictions of the rules (and a race walker would rightly point out that all sports have restrictive rules[2]). The speed with which the elite travel illustrates the point, with the world record for 20 kilometres being just 1 hour 17 minutes and 21 seconds, and for 50 kilometres, 3 hours 35 minutes and 47 seconds. At just under 16 and 14 kilometres per hour respectively, that's considerably faster than most people can run—presuming, of course, most people could run 20 kilometres and 50 kilometres, which they couldn't.

As mentioned above, race walking has a number of rules and regulations like any other sport, but the most important is the one that outlines what constitutes a fair walk. Rule 230.1 of the International Association of Athletic Federations' (IAAF) official regulations (from www.iaaf.org) reads as follows:

> **Race Walking is a progression of steps so taken that the walker makes contact with the ground so that no visible (to the human eye) loss of contact occurs. The advancing leg shall be straightened (i.e. not bent at the knee) from the moment of first contact with the ground until the vertical upright position.**

---

to say it was one double entendre after another, most of them the same one regarding Mrs Slocombe's pussy (cat).

2   One race-walking website makes the comparison to swimming. Freestyle, it points out, is the fastest swimming stroke, yet competitions are held for slower strokes like butterfly and backstroke. What's the difference, it asks, the subtext pleading, 'So leave us alone, okay?'

In other words, a race walker must always have some part of one foot on the ground at all times, and his legs must not be bent when they pass under his body; at least as far as the naked eye of officials or judges can discern. And if one of race walking's many judges—who are spread out over the course (usually a street circuit)—sees an infringement of this rule she will silently issue that walker with a warning, colloquially known as a 'red card'.

Of course, just to confuse matters, the word 'warning' is one used by the race walking fraternity even though the infringing walker isn't verbally warned at the time. On spotting an infringement the judge will notify the chief judge, who will ensure that a red card is placed next to the walker's name on a noticeboard which is positioned near the road or track where it can be seen by competitors. The purpose of this is to prevent the walker from knowing which judge issued the warning because the rules also state that no one judge can issue more than one warning to the same walker (to avoid claims of bias). Were a walker aware which judge issued them a warning he could, theoretically, run past this judge next time around while blowing a raspberry.

When a competitor receives a third warning he is disqualified from the race by the chief judge—a heartbreaking thing to discover when you are just about to enter the Olympic Stadium at the end of your 20-kilometre walk, a few hundred metres from the gold medal.[3]

The use of the naked eye to judge walking indiscretions is problematic, not least because a judge can't possibly follow every race walker for every minute

---

3 Australian walker Jane Saville was disqualified in such a manner in the final stages of the 20-kilometre walk at the 2000 Olympic Games in Sydney. Race-leader Saville was about to enter the stadium—where the roar from the home crowd would have all but carried her home—when a judge emerged from the shadows, like a police car from behind a tree, waving a red disc in the air. It was Saville's third and final warning and in her grief she looked disturbingly like the anguished figure in Edvard Munch's *The Scream*.

of the race. For every indiscretion they see, they may have missed many more. Moreover, as today's super slow-motion replays show, race walkers break Rule 230.1 frequently yet escape censure because judges don't have the advantage of freeze frames and slow-motion replays.

Race walking dates back to the seventeenth century, when English footmen (menservants) alternated between running and walking as they accompanied their masters' coaches on long trips. Why they weren't allowed to at least lie on the floor of the cabin so their masters could use them as footstools is not clear. In any case, by the 1700s and 1800s walking competitions were in vogue in England and, along with horse racing, walking—for all its imperfections—was a sport that punters found attractive. A typical race back then was a test of endurance, such as having to walk 100 miles in less than 24 hours.

In 1866 a 7-mile walking race on a track was introduced to the British athletic championships and in 1908, walking made its debut at the Olympic Games in London, in the form of both a 3500-metre and a 10-mile race. Walking races of varying distances remained in the Olympics until and including 1924, when the sport was dropped due to what were seen as its irregularities. But in 1932 it was re-introduced, over a 50-kilometre distance, and by 1952, 20-kilometre and 50-kilometre distances became standard. Women would have to wait until 1992 for women's race walking to debut at Olympic level.

Such has been the chequered history of race walking that further changes to the sport cannot be ruled out. However, it is doubtful the sport's governing bodies will ever bow to the call from the cheap seats of, 'Just run, why don't you?'

It **sounds suspiciously** like a Monty Python skit, but retro running, or backwards running, is a growing athletic movement. While most often used as a training tool for more conventional forms of running that don't usually induce anxiety about banging into sign posts or speeding whitegoods vans, retro running is also practised in race format over varying distances and terrains. In 2006, what's believed to be the first ever long-distance, up-hill retro-running race took place in Switzerland, with the route being an 11-kilometre track up Stanserhorn Mountain in the Swiss Alps[1].

Although athletes may well have been experimenting with backwards running for a long time (1926–28 world heavyweight boxing champion Gene Tunney is said to have undertaken a daily backwards run of a few miles while throwing

---

1 Swiss social worker Rinaldo Inäbnit—who raced with a rear-view mirror—won in a time of 2 hours 43 minutes.

punches), retro running as a growing trend dates back to the late 1970s. It was around this time that some backward-thinking physiotherapists and trainers began recommending it to injured athletes with knee and back problems, believing it had less impact on the body than forwards running (notwithstanding the increased risk of collisions or falls). Research, such as that conducted by the University of Oregon, suggests backwards running not only reduces strain on the joints and helps strengthen abdominal and back muscles, but that retro runners only need move at 80 cent of the speed of forward runners to receive the same physiological and fitness benefits. Perhaps as a result, most modern sporting teams include retro-running exercises in their training regimens.[2]

While retro running does appear to be physically beneficial, it's arguably the novelty factor that has helped its rise in popularity among the fitness set— who, if aerobics is any indication (and surely it is), are notoriously prone to boredom. That said, many take it as seriously as one can, and races have been held around the world and records have been broken almost as fast as they can be written down. These records,[3] at the time of writing, included:

Men's 100 m: 13.6 seconds, set by Ferdie Ato Adoboe of Ghana in 1991

Men's 200 m: 32.38 seconds, set by Roland Wegner of Germany in 2004

Men's 400 m: 1 minute 9.56 seconds, set by Thomas Dold of Germany in 2005

Men's 1500 m: 5 minutes 53 seconds, by Michele Ermacora of Italy in 2004

----

2 Experts suggest backwards running—undertaken in short bursts at a comfortable speed and well away from obstacles—works well as part of a cool down after regular exercise. Go slowly and take small steps at first. Let the ball of the foot contact first then allow the heel to touch briefly.

3 From www.recordholders.org.

Men's marathon (42.195 km): 3 hours 43 minutes 39 seconds, set by Xu Zhenjun of China in 2004

Trans-USA: Arvind Pandya of India walked backwards from Los Angeles to New York (5,100 km) in 107 days in 1984

Longest distance: Plennie Wingo of the United States walked backwards from Santa Monica, California, to Istanbul, Turkey (13,000 km) in 1931/32

Women's 100 m: 17.80 seconds, set by Simone Kühn of Austria in 2006

Women's 200 m: 43.5 seconds, by Marjorie Isaks of South Africa in 2004

Women's 400 m: 1 minute 32.85 seconds, set by Claudia Wirth of Germany in 2006

Women's mile: 7 minutes 34 seconds, by Stefania Zambello of Italy in 1998

Women's marathon: 6 hours 5 minutes 42 seconds, set by Paula Mairer of Austria in 2004 (run on a 400-metre track)

Other 'backward' sports

HIGH JUMP

In the early days of the high jump, athletes used to dive forwards over the bar as though they were jumping out the window of a burning building. Following that, the scissor kick and straddle jump came into vogue. But then, at the 1968 Olympic Games in Mexico, US athlete Dick Fosbury introduced the world to his signature backwards leap—which won him a gold medal—now known

---

as the Fosbury Flop. Starting from an acute angle, Fosbury approached the bar at a run before turning his body sideways, leaping off his outside foot and going over the bar backwards, arching his back as he went. The Fosbury Flop is now used almost exclusively by high jumpers around the world.

ROWING

From little aluminium and inflatable row boats to long, sleek racing shells used in rowing regattas, oar-propelled boats are almost always powered by people facing in the opposite direction to where they want to go. The backwards technique, though seemingly counter-intuitive, allows a rower to use her legs to help drive her stroke, making her progress significantly easier.

BACKSTROKE

Performed by the un-practised, backstroke is one of the ugliest swimming strokes and it imbues the swimmer with an unnatural fear of slamming the top of her hand against the tiles at the end of the pool even when good sense tells her she's nowhere near it. On the other hand, with the swimmer facing up, breathing is easier and the views of vast blue skies can be dreamy. The backstroke is the only competition swimming style where the swimmer starts in the water.

TUG OF WAR

An actual Olympic sport between 1900 and 1920, tug of war (or tug o' war) pits two teams, equal in number and weight, against each other in a contest of strength.[4] Each team places itself along either end of a long thick rope marked with a centre line (which, at the start of the contest, must be positioned directly above a mark on the ground) and two other lines 4 metres either side of that. When the tug commences each team pulls and attempts to march backwards in order to haul the opposition towards them so that the marking on the rope closest to the opposition crosses the centre line marked on the ground. If they do that, or if a member of the opposition falls or sits down, they win. Although tug of war is a game played at picnics and the kind of corporation team-building days that make almost everyone feel squirmy, many take it very seriously and compete regularly in events overseen by the Tug of War International Federation (TWIF).

GOANNA-PULLING

Not nearly as deviant as it sounds, goanna-pulling is a form of tug of war between two people practised at Wooli in the Northern Rivers region of New South Wales, Australia. The name derives from the fact that both contestants have to be on all fours, facing each other, on the ground when attempting to pull their opponent backwards over a mark on the ground by the thick leather

---

4 A unverifiable story states that on 25 October 1997, 1600 people in Taiwan took part in a mass game of tug of war in celebration of Retrocession Day (an annual observance to commemorate the end of 50 years of Japanese colonial rule on October 25, 1945). The strain snapped the rope, and the resulting whiplash severed the arms of two men beneath the shoulder.

strap looped around both their necks. In doing so they inevitably raise their heads, arch their backs and scramble around with their legs and arms looking for purchase. Just like goannas would do if they were playing tug of war with each other—something never noted, not even by the late Steve Irwin, who was always happy to stick his head down a dark hole in the name of 'Crikey! Have a go at that! She's got me nose between her razor-sharp teeth. Isn't she beauuuuuutiful!' The Goanna-Pulling Championships have a number of weight divisions and are held annually over the Easter long weekend.

ROCK, Paper, Scissors

As a way to settle arguments, 'pistols at ten paces' certainly had its drawbacks, not least possible death for one, if not both, of the warring parties. There could be no such criticism levelled at rock, paper, scissors, one of the simplest and safest dispute settlers (or selection methods) ever devised.

Ostensibly a child's game, rock, paper, scissors is played around the world with its name varying accordingly.[1] Though it appears to be a game based

---

1 In the Western world it is also known as paper, rock, scissors. Around the world it is known as *ching, chong, cha* (South Africa); *schnick, schnack, schnuck* (Germany); *piedra, papel, tijeras* (Spain) and *chin, chan, pu* (Mexico). In some countries the symbols are different. An Indonesian version, for example, features an elephant, a person and an ant, represented, respectively, by a thumb, first finger and little finger. In terms of hierarchy, the elephant can crush the person, the person can crush the ant, and the ant can overcome the elephant—by crawling into its ear and driving it crazy.

entirely on luck—like the toss of a coin, but more interactive—connoisseurs of the game speak of psychology, tactics and gambits which, they believe, are all particularly applicable when something is known of one's opponent. The premise behind this is that no one's behaviour is entirely random and that if you know someone (or have at least played rock, paper, scissors against them many times) then you can learn to predict how she might play the game.

Some regard the game so seriously that rock, paper, scissors societies and clubs have been formed. One organization, the World RPS Society in Canada, has hosted an annual world championship since 2002. Hundreds of people from around the world have taken part in the championships, which offer upwards of C$7000 as a first prize (the US national championships offered a US$50,000 prize in 2007). Canada's reluctance to get involved in wars and its fondness for the benign rock, paper, scissors may be more than just coincidence.

Rock, paper, scissors involves two people simultaneously shaping one of their hands into the eponymous objects. This is known as the 'throw' and it's the result of bringing one's fist down in a hammering motion so that it stops and opens into the chosen symbol just before the arm is perpendicular to the body.[2] A rock is formed by a clenched fist; paper is formed by an open hand, palm down; and scissors are formed by the extension of the index and middle fingers so that they resemble scissors. Each of the three symbols beats one of the other two. That is, rock 'smashes' scissors, paper 'covers' rock, scissors 'cut' paper.[3] Anyone looking to apply logic to such evaluations is bound to get upset, so best not to.

----

2 The RPS Society writes that 'players must reveal their chosen throw to their opponent prior to reaching the 90-degree mark. Any throw delivered past this critical point must be considered a forced rock'.

3 If both players select the same symbol the game is considered tied and another round is played. Rock, paper, scissors is usually played as a 'best-of-three' scenario. Often, in losing two games in a row, a competitor might pressure her

In order to make the game as fair as possible the two competitors must agree upon how to reach the moment of the throw. Typically a count occurs, during which the competitors bring their fists up and down in time with the count. Thus, 'One, two, (throw)' as done in the United States, or 'One, two, three, (throw)' as done in Australia, or some similar variation. This is known as the 'prime'. If at any time players are not in sync with their primes then play must stop. Accomplished cheats may deliberately fall slightly behind in the prime to allow a quick adjustment of their throw as they may get a split second to estimate what sort of throw their opponent might make.

All attempts at cheating aside, rock, paper, scissors has the appearance of being a luck-based game. Not so, some say. For one thing, some experienced players like to think they can predict what someone may throw by her body language (in poker, this is called a 'tell'); perhaps she holds her elbow lower when she throws a rock, or she blinks frequently when a scissors is on its way. Other experienced players like to apply personality types to the different symbols. Accordingly, paper is subtle and the choice of intelligent, passive–aggressive types. Scissors are sneaky and malicious in a calculated way, while rocks are bludgeons, preferred by beginners and those who find themselves in trouble.

Further to such insights, seasoned rock, paper, scissors players sometimes like to employ predetermined throw sequences (presuming a best of three contest) called 'gambits' in order to overwhelm an opponent with psychology. Then again, the impression of a gambit might be enough. Start off with two rocks and your opponent might be expecting a third on the premise that you

---

opposite to make it a best-of-five contest instead. If she loses the first three she may then suggest best of seven. And so on. Such a competitor is quite possibly an only child.

are using the avalanche (see below) and accordingly pull out paper—but you expect that and throw scissors. Bam!

For everyone else, rock, paper, scissors remains a simple game and the perfect way to determine whose turn it is to put out the garbage, one of life's thorniest issues.

Rock, Paper, Scissors —Best known gambits[4]

The Avalanche: Three rocks in succession. 'A relentless and devastating offensive maneuver, which requires bravado bordering on recklessness to execute'.

The Bureaucrat: Paper, paper, paper. 'The ultimate in passive–aggressive play.'

The Crescendo: Paper, scissors, rock. 'The slow-building nature of this gambit makes it a very elegant opening series. The devastating rock is the coup de grâce.'

The Denouement: Rock, scissors, paper. 'The mirror of the Crescendo and uses a cooling-down approach. When used in tandem with the Crescendo the result is often a baffled opponent.'

---

4 Quoted material taken from the World RPS Society's website
   (www.worldrps.com).

Fistful o' Dollars: Rock, paper, paper. 'The rapid switch from offensive to defensive play can force an opponent into a vulnerable spot.'

Paper Dolls: Paper, scissors, scissors. 'Paper levels the playing field and is followed by a couple of quick and sneaky Scissors, which makes it an extremely effective gambit against the unwary.'

Scissor Sandwich: Paper, scissors, paper. 'An invasive and devious gambit. While not the most offensive of the gambits, its main purpose is to unsettle the opponent through use of the concealed Scissors.'

The Toolbox: Scissors, scissors, scissors. 'Requires steady hands and steely nerves. Given the puerile popularity of Rock, this gambit is not suggested for use against beginners.'

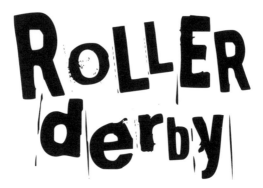

After the invention of roller skates in the mid 1700s, something akin to a scientific law of nature was immediately noted: seeing someone swan about on wheels arouses not only admiration but, conversely, an overwhelming desire to wipe the smile off her stupid face by knocking her over. The sport of roller derby appears to be predicated on such a law.

Mostly played in the United States, at both professional and amateur level, a roller derby is a contact sport in which two teams of five people roller-skate around an oval track, attempting to accrue points by lapping members of the opposing team. Their efforts are made more difficult by opposition skaters who can impede their progress—if not draw it to a dramatic and crowd-pleasing halt—with a bodycheck and, in some cases, a judiciously drawn elbow. For this reason skaters wear helmets, mouth guards and a variety of pads to protect their bones and, in only a minority of cases, their looks.[1]

---

1 Many skaters in roller derbies tend to have the kind of faces you'd expect to find

A roller derby begins with both teams assembling together, as a pack, on the track. Within each team, players assume a number of designated roles, usually as four blockers and one jammer—with one of the blockers also acting as a pivot. At the referee's signal what's known as a 'jam' commences and the respective pivots scoot out in front of the rolling pack and set the pace. The two opposing jammers, however, hang back until another signal from the referee. When that comes they catch up to the pack, navigate through it, and race ahead so that they again come to the rear of the pack.

Scoring commences when the jammers manage to get through the pack on this second attempt. One point is scored for each blocker on the opposing team passed by a jammer. Blockers, meantime, attempt to prevent opposing jammers from passing, while at the same time helping their own jammers get through the pack. They do this by impeding the opposition jammer (which is a nice way of saying ramming them) and, when they can manage it, pushing or flinging their own jammer forwards as if from a slingshot. The first jammer to get through the pack becomes the lead jammer and may call off the jam at any time. The jam concludes after two minutes, or when the lead jammer calls off the jam for strategic reasons. Until then, jammers are allowed to lap the pack time and again.

Considering the above state of play you'd have to imagine that many spectators, and possibly even many players, have absolutely no idea what is going on—despite the different helmet designs and colours for blockers and jammers. That being the case, fans are content to get their kicks simply by seeing competitors knock the cusses out of each other. Although competitors are not usually allowed to punch or trip each other, roller derbies can be

----

under a hessian sack that has eyeholes cut into it—and that's just the women. Whether it's the sport that has made them this way, or that only people with nothing to lose aesthetically decide to play the sport, is difficult to say.

bloody affairs. Depending on the competition or league, however, sometimes the violence (if not the match) is stage-managed along the lines of professional wrestling. In such leagues you may see two rival skaters with personae to match their nom de plumes brawling off court.

The history of the roller derby—which developed out of a roller-skating endurance race invented in 1935—is as long and convoluted as the plot history of *Days of Our Lives*. In short, the halcyon days of roller derbies were in the late 1940s and 1950s, when derbies were well attended and mainstream television provided regular coverage. The sport continued into the 1960s, by which time a number of rival leagues had sprung up ('Roller Derby' was always a proper noun for a specific league or competition, but today it's usually accepted as a generic description of the sport as a whole). After spluttering through the next few decades, roller derbies experienced a low-level renaissance and today a number of competitions exist in the United States (the United Kingdom, Australia and New Zealand also have leagues) with some of the most high-profile being all-female leagues.

That little girls all over the United States now have the opportunity to grow up to be hatchet-faced roller girls in teams such as the Texas Rollergirls' Hell Marys can only be seen as a victory for equal opportunity.

Skating of a different kind

GROUP SKATING

A kind of *passeggiata*[2] on wheels, group skating is an organized, though non-competitive, activity where large groups of people regularly gather to skate through a city—either on old-style roller skates or, more often, in-line skates.

Europe has embraced the group skate idea. Parisians are particularly keen, if the Friday night Pari Roller is any indication. Said to attract the largest number of skaters in the world (more than 20,000 have been known to participate in a single night), the Pari Roller is an approximately 30-kilometre skate beginning at 10 pm every clement Friday evening at Place Raoul Dautry in the fourteenth arrondissement. Every week the route differs and it's so organized that skaters are led by police on motorbike, accompanied by more police on skates, and trailed by two ambulances in case of any accidents. As the race is designed for confident skaters (cobblestones and downhills are tackled, reasonably high

---

2 An Italian custom still hanging in there today, *la passeggiata* is a slow walk before supper, where families, friends, lovers and all sorts stroll through the streets, often arm in arm, chatting, joking, licking gelato and watching the passing parade of people doing the same. It's a wonderful custom that works best in tightly knit cities with piazzas and pedestrian-friendly lanes. Relatively modern cities, enslaved by motor vehicles, are not so amenable to people actually using their legs to get around, let alone being happy to do so. A *passeggiata* in a car, in that case, is known as a traffic jam.

speeds are maintained), organizers ask that participants wear protective gear and know how to brake. It is definitely not suitable for those who skate in a position resembling someone reluctantly peering over the edge of an abyss.

Organizers consider the skate a 'freedom ride', where participants (who are encouraged to make a financial contribution to the running of the event) get to discover the city from an unusual vantage point, meet other people and enjoy the wind running through their hair.[3]

Other major cities have their own version of the Pari Roller. Berlin has a Sunday skate night, while London, Munich, Amsterdam, Tokyo and Buenos Aires have their own events.

MARATHONS

On the same day that Berlin hosts its annual marathon (42.195 kilometres) for runners, the city also holds a skate marathon for inline- and roller-skaters—on a course that finishes with competitors skating through the iconic Brandenburg Gates. With about 8,000 skaters taking part every year, it must be one of the world's most popular marathons for skaters. Many other cities throughout the world (such as Havana, Buenos Aires, Vienna, Rome and New York) also hold skate marathons.

---

3 Yes, Pari Roller participants are encouraged to wear helmets. But are young skaters, full of *joie de vivre* and an intoxicating sense of invincibility, always going to cover their beautiful dos with lumps of horrid plastic? *Non!*

SAUNA Sitting

More a display of masochism than a sport, sauna sitting is an endurance event where competitors willingly see how long they can remain inside a sauna that is hot enough to cook a monkey.

Sauna sitting is, of course, the kind of thing people with access to a sauna are wont to do when feeling daring. It's particularly, and perversely, attractive to children and teenage boys when they are staying with their families at hotels. Having slipped away from their parents, who are only too happy to see the back of them, they pile into the sauna, turn up the thermostat as high as it can go, and proceed to pour water over the scalding rocks until their tiny brains start to reduce like a fine cooking sauce. When they can stand it no more they bolt outside and, screaming with anticipatory delight, jump straight into the hotel pool and, in doing so, terrorize its sole occupant, usually a curmudgeonly senior citizen who moments earlier couldn't believe he had the pool to himself and for the first time in his life thought himself almost happy.

Practised around the world, sauna sitting is surely most popular in and around Scandinavia, where sauna use borders on the ritualistic. More precisely, it's in Finland—a country of 5.1 million people and 1.7 million saunas—where the amateur pastime of sauna sitting has been elevated from the kind of thing some do for a dare into codified competition, namely the Sauna World Championships, which have been held annually in the lakeside town of Heinola since 1999.

Though far from an athletic pursuit, sauna sitting tests a person's pain threshold like few other activities—even a Mariah Carey music marathon. The world championship, which begins with two days of elimination rounds (commonly called heats, though to refer to them as such in this instance might appear to be a bad pun, so it will be avoided), challenges competitors to sit in a sauna the temperature of which is set to 110 degrees Celsius. The discomfort level (and humidity) is then increased every 30 seconds when water is thrown over the stove.

Through it all, competitors are not allowed to disturb their fellow competitors, which means no talking and certainly no towel flicking. All they are allowed to do is give the thumbs up every so often so that medical officers standing by know they aren't on the verge of a heart attack.[1] The winner is the last person to stay inside the sauna and walk out unaided. And when he does so, he will find himself before a grandstand of some 1500 spectators who are drinking beer, eating sausages and thinking how delighted they are not to be inside that sauna.

---

1   Competitors tend to take on the appearance of rare roast beef. This is because blood flow to the skin increases and blood vessels expand to meet the demand. In hot temperatures, such as in a sauna set to comfortable levels, blood flows through the skin up to forty times faster than usual. In the Heinola sauna it's closer to fifty times, which means competitors' hearts are fairly galloping.

Considering the danger involved, it's hardly a surprise that all contestants must sign legal waivers before competing in the event, lest they cook one of their organs or, worse, drop dead. But such dangers haven't dissuaded people from signing up and competitors are said to come from around the world—although the Finns, it seems, are near unbeatable. Since the competition began, Finns have won all eight men's titles and five out of eight women's titles, with the longest time endured inside being 16 minutes 15 seconds—a record achieved by Finn Timo Kaukonen in 2003.

Other endurance activities

HANDS ON A HARD BODY CONTEST

Like sauna sitting—which even the most flexible definition of sport would struggle to include—Texas' Hands on a Hard Body competition certainly requires endurance, fortitude and desperation in equal measures. Held annually between 1992 and 2005, the contest, which sounds like something you might see at an adult expo, involves standing with a hand pressed flush against the body of a brand new Nissan 4WD for the longest possible time without leaning. The person who lasts longest gets to keep the vehicle.

Each year 24 contestants are chosen to compete after their names are drawn from a barrel at a Nissan dealership in Longview, Texas. Contestants traditionally have to hold out for days to have a chance of victory. In 2000,

---

the winner had to maintain his poise and pose for 126 hours, which is an astounding 5 days 6 hours.

Despite a 5-minute break every hour and a 15-minute break every 6 hours, the contest is punishing and it takes both a physical and psychological toll on competitors,[2] who, it must always be remembered, have volunteered to take part in an event that could well meet the definition of torture. Blood pressure rises, ankles begin to resemble the legs of a billiard table and the mind wanders, with hallucinations not uncommon. But through it all competitors must keep their positions or be disqualified. As 1994 winner Benny Perkins says in a 1997 documentary film named after the contest, 'If you can't hunt with the big dogs, you get up on the porch with the puppies.'

2 A tragedy at the 2005 contest saw that contest draw to an immediate halt, and the 2006 contest cancelled altogether (its future is still in doubt). Forty-eight hours into the contest, twenty-four-year old Ricky Vega had had enough and lifted his hand, forgoing his chance of walking away with the new vehicle. He then strolled across the street, threw a garbage can through the window of a Kmart, and entered the store. Shortly after, while still in the store, he killed himself with a shotgun and shells, which he found in the sporting department. It was thought that sleep deprivation may have interfered with his judgment.

SEPAK takraw loosely translates as 'kick volleyball' but the sport, when played by the elite, has more than a touch of a martial art about it as well. Suffice to say that you could throw your average takraw champion out of a ten-storey window and he'd more than likely land on his feet, completely unscathed, counting the pocket full of butterflies he caught on the way down.[1]

Widely played in Southeast Asia, *sepak takraw*, or *takraw* for short, is a seemingly simple sport that has been elevated to a virtual art form by the athleticism of its players. In essence, *takraw* is a game of three-on-three (or sometimes two-on-two) volleyball played with the feet and, to a lesser extent, the head, knees, chest and shoulders. Three touches are allowed before a team must return the grapefruit-sized ball—either a hard plastic or woven

---

1 On the off chance he *won't* land on his feet, however, it's best not to test the theory and instead take it as read.

rattan ball—over the net. Unlike in volleyball, one player can make all three touches. As the game's name suggests, no player is allowed to use his hands in general play, although a player is permitted to use his hands to assist in a service, which he does by tossing the ball to a team-mate who must volley it (kick it on the full) over the net and into the opposition's half of the court.

At 13.4 metres by 6.1 metres, a *sepak takraw* court is about the size of a doubles badminton court—although court size may vary when the game is played socially on dirt or grass, as it often is. The net that divides the court stands 1.52 metres for men and 1.42 metres for women; high enough to provide a challenge but low enough to allow *takraw* players to return the ball with acrobatic élan.

A service is an elegant action to watch.[2] A competitor rotates his leg like a windmill blade, keeping it straight as he strokes the ball at head height. But it's *takraw's* equivalent of the volleyball spike that is particularly impressive. With a player having set up the spike with a ball lobbed to above the height of the net, his team-mate jumps into the air, inverting his entire body. Upside-down he still has the presence of mind to kick the ball *down* into the opposition's court, a most difficult shot to counter (although an opposition player will have invariably jumped in the air himself in attempting to get his foot in the right place for a block). That done, instead of landing on his back and neck—as soccer players tend to do after executing a similar move called a bicycle kick—he continues to twist his body so he lands on all fours.

The sport of *sepak takraw* is thought to have its roots in Malaysia in the 1500s, although other nations, like Thailand, lay some claim to inventing it. In one version of events, it evolved from *sepak raga* (*sepak* meaning 'kick' and

---

2 … as well as being wince-inducing to the average spectator, who is in danger of pulling a hamstring when merely bending over to tie his shoelaces.

raga describing the traditional woven rattan ball), a game in which players stood in a circle and tried to keep the *raga* in the air for as long as possible using only their feet. Variations of this were also played in other Southeast Asian countries. In Thailand it was called *takraw* (the Thai word for the rattan ball), in the Philippines, *sepa sepa*, in Myanmar, *ching loong*, in Indonesia, *rago* and in Laos, *kator*.

Although a game resembling traditional *sepak raga* is still played today,[3] at some point the game went in another direction taking on the dimensions of a court, a net and a scoring system similar to that of volleyball (best of three sets, first to twenty-one in each set wins). The new game, which came to be known as *sepak takraw*, became wildly popular in Southeast Asia and in 1960 a standard set of rules and regulations was established. Today, the sport continues to grow in popularity and it is contested at the biannual Southeast Asian Games and the quadrennial Asian Games, and it will be played at the inaugural Asian Beach Games in 2008. Before the Asian Games, *takraw's* highest-profile tournament has traditionally been the King's Cup World Championships held annually in Bangkok.

---

3 One such game is hoop *takraw* where players not only stand in a circle and attempt to keep the ball airborne as creatively as they can, but also knock it through a basket with three hoops suspended in the air.

Something Similar

FOOTBAGGING

A footbag[4] is a mandarin-sized sack with a soft filling (polystyrene balls, sand and rice are common), which is juggled, primarily with the feet, by one or more people. Footbagging appears to be particularly popular among the alternative-lifestyle set, which is a blessing since the more time such people spend kicking around a footbag means the less time they are sitting in a group, preposterously straight-faced, beating bongo drums.

While most footbagging takes place within informal groups to pass the time, there are regimented games such as circle kicking (in which participants form a circle and move the footbag around it from person to person), freestyle (in which a solo player keeps the footbag in the air as creatively as possible, mainly using the lower lace area, instep and outside of a shoe) and footbag net. The latter closely resembles *sepak takraw*, as it is played on a badminton-sized court with a 1.52-metre net. Unlike in *takraw*, only one kick is allowed per turn.

JIANZI

Another sport similar to *sepak takraw* is *jianzi*, also known as 'shuttlecock' since the projectile in use is a type of shuttlecock; in this case a flat rubber

----

----

4 Footbagging is frequently referred to as Hacky Sack, which is not always correct. Hacky Sack is a trade name referring to a particular brand of footbag.

disc out of which shoot a number of long feathers. Played on a court and with rules similar to badminton, *jianzi* requires competitors to use only their feet to keep the shuttlecock in play. As with footbagging and *sepak takraw*, flexibility is advantageous and many players have mastered a smash shot executed by raising one leg above their head and batting the shuttlecock down using the sole of their shoe.

Jianzi is said to have originated in China in the fifth century BC, but it wasn't until *jianzi* was demonstrated at the 1936 Berlin Olympics that it began to be played around the world. In 1999, the International Shuttlecock Foundation was formed and world championships are now contested annually.

An apparent contradiction in terms, speed golf is a sport that involves completing eighteen holes of a golf course in the lowest combination of strokes and time. Although it does mean players get to the bar considerably sooner than they normally would, the very idea of running to play golf is enough to chill the big bones of golf's more portly legions who ordinarily struggle for breath doing any form of exercise, be it brushing their teeth or towelling themselves after a shower.

The basic difference between regular golf and speed golf is that in the latter version of the game players run between strokes and spend next to no time deliberating over shots, let alone taking half a dozen practice swings, tossing sprigs of grass into the air to judge the wind, and breaking irons over their knee. The reason for this is that in speed golf the time it takes a player to complete his round is added to the number of strokes he took. For instance, shooting a round of 90 in 51 minutes would give a player a speed golf score of 141. Professional golfers, by contrast, take 4–5 hours to complete a round.

It is thought that American middle-distance runner Steve Scott—who was curious to discover how quickly he could complete a round of golf—first played speed golf in 1979. Carrying only a single club—a three-iron—he raced around a Californian course in 29 minutes and 30 seconds, taking 95 shots (which would be scored today as 124.30). He must surely have discovered that his unusual endeavour made running more engaging and golf more like real exercise.

Since Scott's breakthrough round, speed golf (also known as 'extreme golf', 'golf on the run' and 'hit and run golf') has gained in popularity, although its very nature means it doesn't go down well at your average golf course and, consequently, remains a niche sport. Unless a special tournament has been put on, speed golfers can only ply their unique trade on a regular golf course, which means they must effectively be the first to tee off in the morning or else they'll risk upsetting the members who don't like their comparatively sloth-like movements rubbed in their faces.

Without a formal organizing body, speed golf has no uniform set of rules, although it's generally understood that in most instances speed golfers adhere to the rules and etiquette of golf. Thus, besides not having to remove the flagstick when putting, a speed golfer is expected to replace divots, rake bunkers and accept penalty strokes, such as when he loses a ball or hits a moving ball—as he may be tempted to do on the putting green.

Although Scott played with a single club during speed golf's maiden round, there is still no limit to how many, or how few, clubs a speed golfer must carry (although you need at least one). For obvious reasons, however, a speed golfer strives to minimize the weight he must carry from hole to hole. As such, speed golfers tend to carry lightweight, junior-style golf bags with as few as six clubs, including a putter, a driver and a wedge. Ordinarily a regular golfer carries (or has carried for him, which gives some hint as to why many golfers are over par when it comes to their waist measurement) about fourteen clubs.

Interestingly, the speed with which speed golfers play doesn't appear to overly affect their regular game, with most reports suggesting the extra haste adds a mere two or three strokes to a player's usual score. One explanation for this is that a speed golfer's desire for haste doesn't allow him to think too much—a terrible habit among golfers that so often leads to trouble, hence the explanatory phrase 'paralysis by analysis'.

Comparing speed golf scores is problematic since no two golf courses are the same and can thus vary in total length, with anything from 4–7 kilometres normal. For the record, however, the lowest speed golf score is thought to be 109.06, shot by golf professional Christopher Smith at the Chicago Speed Golf Classic in 2005. Smith shot a superb round of 65 and took just 44 minutes and 6 seconds to do it. If Mark Twain was right in calling golf 'a good walk spoiled', Smith at least got the spoiling over with quickly.

Sport stacking is an activity whereby individuals or teams stack (and unstack) pre-determined sequences of plastic cups so quickly there appears to be some trickery afoot. The activity was formerly known as cup stacking but this was changed in recent years, as it made the sport appear about as appealing as doing the dishes after a family reunion.

Originating in California in the 1980s (after which it received some exposure on US TV's *The Tonight Show* with Johnny Carson), sport stacking received its greatest fillip in 2001 with the formation of a governing body, the World Sport Stacking Association, better known to plastic cup enthusiasts around the world as the WSSA. Today the WSSA works to promote and govern sport stacking,[1]

---

1 According to the WSSA, 'Sport stacking not only develops important physical skills, such as hand–eye coordination, quickness and focus; it also promotes self-confidence, teamwork and good sportsmanship.'

a self-imposed mandate that includes spreading the word that sport stacking is so much more than a domestic chore; it is, in fact, a competitive sport.

At tournaments around the world—but mostly in America, where the WSSA oversees numerous competitions, including annual world championships— sport stackers compete in a number of different disciplines, which vary depending on the number of cups and the sequence of the stack. Each sequence tends to begin with one or more piles of cups turned upside down on a table.

The competitive sequences are:

3-3-3: This sequence uses nine cups, which are arranged in three nested stacks of three (meaning the three cups in each stack are pushed into each other and placed upside down on the table). Having tapped a timer pad in front of them (which starts a digital clock set up for judges and spectators to see) the stacker must build, or 'upstack', three adjacent pyramids of three cups each (that is, two on the bottom, one on top of them) then 'downstack' the cups back into their original stacks. When she's finished she must tap the timer pad again to stop the clock.

3-6-3: This upstack and downstack sequence uses twelve cups and is as above except that the middle stack contains six cups in a 3-2-1 pyramid. This sequence is also used as the first of three sequences in the 'cycle stack'.

6-6: Using twelve cups, the stacker must create two six-cup pyramids then downstack both into a single pile of cups. This sequence is only used as the second of three sequences in the cycle stack.

1-10-1: Using twelve cups that start as a single downstacked pile, the competitor must first take two cups from the top and set them down on each side of the remaining stack of ten. That done she must upstack the remaining ten into a 4-3-2-1 pyramid before grabbing the two single cups and downstacking the lot into nests of 3-6-3. This sequence is only used as the final sequence in the cycle stack.

The cycle stack: As outlined above, this is a combination of three sequences in order: the 3-6-3, the 6-6 and the 1-10-1. As with the 1-10-1, the cycle stack finishes with a downstacked 3-6-3.

It's important to note that only a certain type of cup is suitable for sport stacking.[2] Paper cups, Styrofoam cups, metal cups, clay Indian chai cups, novelty cups from fast food joints, none of them cut the mustard—in competition at least. At sanctioned WSSA competitions, competitors use specially designed cups that do not stick to each other. Made of tough, durable plastic, the cups have a ledge, or step, towards the bottom which prevents them jamming together when nested, allowing a stacker to lift off the top cup without pulling the rest up with it. Just as importantly, WSSA-sanctioned cups have small holes in the bottom. This allows air to pass through the bottom of the cup making stacking fast and easy. Obviously it's important that competitors remember the holes when the pressure of competition has subsided and they are looking for a receptacle from which to enjoy a refreshing, sugar-laden beverage.

Sport stacking is both an individual and team event. In the latter case, teams of two players must complete the sequences above but do so together, with one player using her right hand, the other her left land. This requires considerable practice to ensure they are in sync with one another. Additionally,

---

2 The WSSA endorses, for sale, special training cups (called 'Super Stacks') made of metal. They are designed for pre-competition use when stackers are warming up for their shot at immortality. Or something. In the same way that lifting a donkey over your head will then make doing the same with a cat seem ridiculously easy, the idea is that the extra weight of the metal cups will make the competition cups seem feather-light and even easier to manoeuvre.

there is a relay for four-person teams. In a relay, each member of the team has to complete the particular sequence before the second member begins the same sequence. And so on. The team competes head to head against another team (in a best-of-three scenario) with the first to finish declared the winner.

Although sport stacking is primarily a children's game, WSSA tournaments hold competitions for sport stackers of all ages. Unlike in most sports, however, children appear to be the most successful. With fingers like spider monkeys', the top child competitors have an adroitness and speed that are breathtaking. Spectators could do worse than keep their wallets in their front pockets.

As the legends of Goliath, Samson, Hercules, Atlas and Superman suggest, humankind has always been fascinated by the deeds of men so big and powerful they could never wear clothes bought off the rack without experiencing severe chafing. It could be argued that strongman competitions, held in various guises around the world, are an attempt to tap into that fascination, which still endures today (although perhaps with a little less awe than in previous times[1]).

Strongman competitions tend to be multi-discipline events, which combine tests of strength, endurance, speed and technique, with theatricality. That is, rather than having competitions mimic straightforward weight-lifting contests as they appear in the Olympic Games, strongman competitions tend to involve a

---

1 Being able to lift a heifer calf over your head is all very impressive, and such strength must come in handy when putting luggage into overhead compartments on aircraft, but since the lamentable invention of hand guns and assault rifles, prodigious strength is not quite as vital or intimidating as it once was. The playing field, as it were, has been levelled.

series of weight-bearing—though sadly not Herculean[2]—labours, be it pulling an aircraft down a runway or lifting television-sized rocks onto podiums.

While competitions of strength have been held since time immemorial (the Scottish Highland Games are one example—see page 212), the modern concept has its roots in a 1977 TV series called *The World's Strongest Man*, which aired on US television. While the network has since changed, The World's Strongest Man competition remains an annual event (the first World's Strongest Woman event was held in 2001) with competitors qualifying through various US and international strongman challenges throughout the year. Invariably, man or woman, the competitors have thighs like sausage-casings stuffed with suckling pigs, and shoulders wide enough to cast a shadow over an entire cubicle of accountants.

To date, the most successful competitors have been from Iceland, which may suggest, if only to the ignorant, that there must be so little to do in Iceland that men spend all their time lifting weights in the gym. Jón Páll Sigmarsson[3] was the first to accumulate four titles, the last of which was in 1990. His deeds were matched by another man mountain, Magnús ver Magnússon, who won in 1991, 1994, 1995 and 1996.

To test competitors fully, and to prevent someone dominating by specializing in particular events, the World's Strongest Man features more than a dozen events,

---

2 Sad, yes; surprising, no. After all, Hercules' twelve labours were as follows: to kill the Nemean lion; to kill the Hydra of Lerna; to capture the Ceryneian hind; to capture the Erymanthian boar; to clean the Augean stables; to kill the Stymphalian birds; to kill the Cretan bull; to capture the Diomedes mares; to acquire the girdle of Hippolyte; to capture the cattle of Geryon; to acquire the Golden Apples of the Hesperides; and to capture Cerberus in the Underworld.

3 'There's no point in being alive if you cannot do the deadlift,' is a quote attributed to Sigmarsson, who was prone to such outbursts ('I am a Viking!' is another). In 1993, at the age of thirty-two, Sigmarrson—who knew he had a congenital heart defect—died while performing deadlifts in a gym.

although they may not all be contested at each competition. All involve lifting, pulling or holding up the kind of weights you'd normally use a crane to budge.

These include:

Farmer's walk: Two ridiculously heavy slabs weighing approximately 125 kilograms (that is, marginally heavier than a fashion-conscious young lady's holiday suitcase) are carried in each hand over a set distance with fastest times determining placing.

Fridge carry/Yoke walk: A 415-kilogram yoke, made up of a crossbeam and two weighted uprights (normally refrigerators), is carried across the shoulders over a maximum of 30 metres or 60 seconds, whatever expires first.

Atlas stones: Five round stones weighing 160, 140, 120, 112 and 100 kilograms are lifted in that order onto five podiums, which increase in height every lift.

Africa stone: A 175-kilogram rock, cut into the shape of the titular continent, is carried high on the chest until it can be carried no more.

Plane pulling: With the help of a harness and rope, each competitor pulls an aircraft weighing approximately 70 tonnes across a 30-metre course with the quickest time determining placing.

Fingal's fingers: In this timed event—named after the mythical Celtic warrior Fingal, or Fionn mac Cumhaill (Finn McCool)—athletes have to lift five 5.5-metre-long poles in ascending order of weight (200, 225, 250, 275, 300 kilograms) and flip them over 180 degrees.

Overhead press: Athletes must lift a 115-kilogram wooden log from the ground then raise it overhead as many times as possible in the 75-second time limit. The log is returned back to the floor in a controlled fashion between lifts.

Pillars of Hercules: The competitor stands between two outward-leaning 160-kilogram pillars, while gripping handles that prevent the pillars from falling over to the side. The winner is the competitor who holds the pillars for the longest time.

Scottish Highland Games events

CABER TOSSING

Despite the popularity of kilts, one would have to imagine that folk were light on for entertainment in the Scottish Highlands when caber tossing was devised. Be that as it may, the traditional Scottish athletic event that has non-enthusiasts everywhere uttering, 'Yes, but *why?*' remains the marquee event of any Highland Games.

Requiring prodigious strength and dexterity, caber tossing involves balancing and throwing a long, tapered, heavy wooden pole in such a manner that it pinwheels in the air with the end that was held by the thrower's hands (the lighter end) ending up furthest away from him. This is even harder than it sounds. While there is no standard measurement for a caber (every Highland Games event has its own distinct set[4]) they are usually at least 5 metres long

---

4 A set of cabers might include cabers of varying weights and heights intended for use by top-flight throwers, amateur throwers, female throwers and junior throwers. Generally speaking, the bigger the thrower, the heavier and longer the

----

and weigh a minimum of 35 kilograms. Not the sort of thing nature ever intended to spin in the air, outside cyclone season at least.

A caber toss begins with a number of officials lowering a caber (heavy end up) into a thrower's cupped hands. When the thrower is ready, the officials step away and the thrower's first challenge is to keep the caber balanced in a vertical position. When the thrower is ready, he runs forward and tosses the caber with a lifting, flipping action—which may or may not cause his kilt to fly up at the back, thereby satisfying the curiosity of many onlookers. Ideally the thrown caber will spin 180 degrees in the air, landing heavy side down, before its momentum causes it to fall away from the thrower.

Contrary to popular belief, a caber-tossing contest is not decided by the distance a competitor has thrown his caber (which comes from the Gaelic *cabar*, meaning a pole or beam) but rather by how it lands. A perfect throw is when the caber lands heavy end down with the lighter end pointing to twelve o'clock, as judged from the path of the thrower's run. Thus a caber that lands at eleven o'clock will score better than one that lands at ten o'clock. In the event no one manages to flip the caber, the highest score will go to the thrower whose caber came closest to 90 degrees.

If no one even manages to balance the caber it might be more interesting if first prize were then awarded to the thrower with the nicest legs. However, in

----

----

caber. Of course throwers can also be called tossers, although they won't be in this book, for obvious reasons.

such an eventuality, the caber is reduced in size until someone manages to toss it successfully.

THE STONE PUT

Similar to the Olympic shot put, the stone put requires competitors to propel a large stone for distance. Unlike the shot put, the stone put has two sub-categories of competition. The first, the 'Braemar Stone', disallows any kind of run up, while the 'Open Stone' allows any kind of run up, glide or spin, so long as the stone is thrown with its having been held against the competitor's neck.

THE WEIGHT OVER THE BAR

In this event, rather than throw a heavy object (in this case a 25-kilogram weight with a handle) for distance, it is thrown—one handed—for height. As in the high jump, each athlete is allowed three attempts at each height before the bar is raised.

THE SHEAF TOSS

Similar to the weight over the bar in that height is a measure of success, the sheaf toss requires competitors to use a pitchfork to fling a bundle of straw wrapped in a burlap bag over a bar.

Tchoukball

Alarmed at the regular injury toll in all kinds of brutish team-based ball sports, Swiss biologist Dr Hermann Brandt made it his mission in the 1960s to create a team sport that was socially inclusive[1] and hardly more dangerous than, say, canasta played with soft cotton gloves. Tchoukball (pronounced *chewk*-ball) was the result of his considered labours.

With no contact between players (which encourages aggression, Dr Brandt believed), no interceptions allowed (this also encourages aggression and risks dangerous collisions) and no running with the ball (what if someone tripped?),

----

1 Point 1 of the (admirably Utopian) Tchoukball Charter reads:
     'The game excludes any striving after prestige, whether personal or collective.
     On a personal level: The attitude of the player implies respect of every other player, whether on one's own side or in the other team, whether stronger or weaker than one's self.
     The game being open to players of all degrees of competency (constitutional or acquired), one inevitably meets players of every possible category. The respect

tchoukball might appear to be safe because players are too bored to get injured, but that wouldn't do the fast-paced, though unusual, sport justice.

Played on a court 40 metres by 20 metres, the object of tchoukball is to score points by throwing a grapefruit-sized leather ball at either of two angled square frames (situated, like common goals, midway along both end lines), so that the ball rebounds off the frame's trampoline-taut netting and back into the field of play. To score a point the ball must rebound in such a way that the opposition do not catch it on the full before it hits the court surface. Unlike most sports, tchoukball teams do not attack a particular goal, meaning they can score at either end of the field, making quick and direct passing an imperative.

Tchoukball, which was officially introduced in 1970, is played over three 15-minute periods between two teams of nine players, who spread themselves across the court so that attacking and defending both goals is viable. When a team comes into possession of the ball they move the ball in either direction by passing it among one another, ensuring no one player takes more than three steps once she catches an uncontested ball (should she drop it, possession changes hands). A maximum of three passes is allowed before someone must shoot at the frame, which is 90 cm square.

Shooting—and defending the shot—is the most dramatic part of the game, for shooters, like European handball players, tend to leap into the air to make

---

and consideration due to one and all obliges each player to adapt his own conduct (technical or tactical) to the circumstances of the moment.

On a collective level: A result, no matter what, involves no-one's reputation and, above all, allows for no sectarianism. From victory one can derive pleasure and even joy, but never the satisfaction of vainglory. The joy of winning is an encouragement, whereas arrogance in victory carries the seeds of a struggle for prestige which we condemn as giving rise to inter-human conflict of every kind and degree.'

—From Federation Internationale de Tchoukball

their shot, thereby ensuring that the ball will rebound off the frame at a sharp angle, making it more difficult to catch. Commonly, some deception occurs before each shot, providing the attacking team has enough passes up its sleeve. Often one player will leap into the air, shaping to shoot, but lob the ball to a following team-mate, who will shoot instead. The purpose of this is to confuse opposition players who are attempting to get in good positions to catch the ball. If the opposition gets a hand on a rebounding ball but fails to control it, the thrower's team is awarded a point.

The defensive team, who must react like jungle cats in order to catch a ball that is thrown with strength in a downward trajectory, must remain outside a 3-metre diameter semi-circle surrounding each goal. The area it borders is known, somewhat dramatically, as the forbidden zone. Similarly, a thrown ball must clear the forbidden zone if the thrower is to score a point for her team. Unlike in most sports, missing the target altogether concedes a point to the opposition.

Since its formation, the International Tchoukball Federation has endeavoured to spread the good news. And while tchoukball is still widely considered a sport reserved for school physical education lessons, it is played internationally and there are European and world championships, with Taiwan, Switzerland and Great Britain traditionally the strongest nations.

As for the name, it's onomatopoeic. Brandt believed 'tchouk' was the sound a ball makes when it hits a frame. Few would be bothered to argue the point.

Other ball games

FISTBALL

A variant of volleyball, fistball is a game in which players use their fists and arms (no open hands) to hit a ball over a 2-metre-high net and attempt to land it in their opposition's half of the court in such a way that it cannot be returned.

The major differences between fistball and volleyball are that fistball is played on a much larger area (50 metres by 20 metres, usually grass) and that the ball is allowed to bounce between hits. As with volleyball, each team of five players is allowed a maximum of three hits between them before the ball must be returned.

The game—a best-of-three-sets contest, with the first team to twenty points winning each set—is mainly played in northern Europe (Germany, Austria and Switzerland in particular), the United States and South America.

FLOORBALL

Floorball is, in many respects, a dry-land version of ice hockey or bandy (see page 41) played mainly in northern Europe. It is a rink game in which players use light sticks with vented and curved plastic blades to hit a small plastic ball into the opposition's goal, which, as in ice hockey, is situated a few metres in from each end line. At elite levels, floorball players are highly skilled and

----

many can manoeuvre the ball with their sticks in such a way that the ball appears to be stuck on the stick.

Floorball, a fast-paced, moderate-contact sport, is usually played between teams of six players (one of whom is a goalkeeper and not equipped with a stick) over three 20-minute periods. Floorball associations exist in numerous countries and world championships are held every two years, with Sweden winning all six of the men's world titles contested since 1996. In the women's world titles, contested since 1997, Sweden have three titles, Finland two, and Switzerland one.

Floorball started in Sweden in the 1970s but it has its roots in floor hockey, played in the United States since the 1950s. The International Floorball Federation was founded in 1986.

GATEBALL

Similar in part to croquet, gateball is a mallet sport in which two teams look to score points by knocking balls through a series of gates or hoops set into a grass field about the size of a tennis court.

Played between two teams of five (the red team wears tags numbered 1, 3, 5, 7, 9; the white team 2, 4, 6, 8, 10) each player has her own ball, with a number on it that corresponds to her tag number. Taking it in turns according to her individual number, each player attempts to knock her ball through three numbered gates spread across the court (players gain one point for every gate their ball passes through). This must be done in the correct order, before a player attempts to hit a goal pole in the centre of the court (for which she earns two points).

Play begins with all ten players lined up outside the court. Player 1 steps up to the mark and attempts to hit her ball through gate 1. If she succeeds, her ball stays where it came to rest while player 2 attempts to hit her ball through gate 1, and so on. Each stroke must be taken within 10 seconds and a game lasts 30 minutes, after which time the cumulative points for each team are compared to determine a winner.

GOALBALL

Devised in 1946 to help the rehabilitation of Second World War veterans who had suffered injuries to their eyes, goalball is a team game played by athletes who are blind or visually impaired. It is the only team sport for visually impaired athletes contested at the Paralympics.

Played on an 18-metre by 9-metre court, goalball is played between two teams of three players who attempt to roll a ball into their opponent's goal— which spans the width of the pitch. To help players identify the whereabouts of the 1.25-kilogram rubber ball, the ball has eight holes and a number of small bells inside it and sounds a little like Santa's sleigh. All players wear eyeshades (thus players with some sight are not advantaged over players who are completely blind), which means that identifying the ball relies entirely on aural clues.

Using pieces of string taped to the floor, players orientate themselves in their respective zones within a few metres of the goal they are defending. Teams (and team-mates within teams) take it in turns to roll the ball towards their opponent's goal after the referee has called 'play'. The defending team players, who also must stay within their zone, attempt to keep the ball out of their goal, usually by lying full stretch on the ground, their arms and legs extended. If they communicate well and orientate themselves correctly, they can cover most of the 9-metre-wide goal.

KICKBALL

A popular US playground game that is increasingly played by adults in semi-ironic recreational leagues—which are as much about beer-based socializing as athletic endeavour—kickball effectively follows the rules of baseball except for the type of ball used and the method of hitting it. In kickball a pitcher rolls (or 'flings' if the game has a competitive edge) an inflatable rubber ball (at least 25 centimetres in diameter) towards a 'batter' who attempts to kick it into the field of play—which is similar in design to a softball/baseball field. Should she swing and miss, a strike will be called (three strikes and she's out); should she kick the ball, she must run to at least first base. Unlike the batter, fielders can use their hands. If they catch a kicked ball on the full, the batter is out. Fielders can also throw a fielded ball to a team-mate standing on any of the bases in order to run out a batter. According to the World Adult Kickball Association, with perhaps a hint of desperation, 'All the cool kids are doing it!' Presumably they mean playing kickball. Not, well, doing *it*.

WALLYBALL

In Australia, 'wally' is a colloquialism for a silly person, someone not too quick on the uptake who has a propensity to do stupid—though mostly harmless— things. Unfortunately, 'wallyball' does not reference that colloquialism. It is in fact an amalgamation of the words wall and volleyball. Not surprisingly then, wallyball is effectively volleyball played on a racquetball court. The result is that there is no 'out', as the ball is still in play when it rebounds off the side or end walls.

Wallyball is played between teams of two, three or four players and rules are similar to those of volleyball. For example, each team is allowed three touches before the ball must be returned over the 2-metre-high net that divides the court in two. But the ball used is rubber (as opposed to the leather or synthetic ball used in volleyball) and players are allowed to deliberately rebound shots off the side walls.

The game is played mostly in the US Midwest, where cold winters drive volleyball players indoors, and many other people crazy.

Many sports and games attract the adjective 'explosive' as a means of describing the action. Only one, however, can use the term in its literal sense, and that's the Colombian game of *tejo*.

Thought to have been around for hundreds of years, *tejo* (pronounced tay-kho) is played in parks, along roadsides, and in bars where it is almost always accompanied by booming music and enough beer, or the anise-flavoured local firewater, *aguardiente*, to either steady the aim or throw it completely out the window. Popular among the working class, *tejo* has similarities to such games as horseshoes, except for the thrilling fact that a successful throw is rewarded by an explosion from a tiny blasting cap; a great incentive to practise if there ever was one.

Typically, *tejo* is played on a flat strip of dirt or clay long enough to place two targets at a challenging distance from each other—anything from 5–15 metres is customary. Targets are commonly small boxes (placed at a 45-degree angle) filled with clay or wet dirt. Within the clay is a metal cylinder, the circumference of which surrounds four small blasting caps—paper sachets of gunpowder called *mechas* (fuses)—which sit on top of the clay.

Individuals or teams, who begin the game by standing in front of one of the target boxes, take turns lobbing heavy metal discs called *tejos* at the target box opposite. Each player throws his respective *tejo*—which is shaped like a small dinner roll—then players swap ends and throw towards the box they started from. Every time a thrower sets off a *mecha*, which makes a satisfying bang and emits a small flash of light, he gains points for himself or his team. Landing a *tejo* in the box without setting off an explosion also earns points. The game is usually played to nine or twenty-one points.

Despite appearances, *tejo* is more than an excuse to make some noise, get drunk, place a bet and, ultimately, get into a fight—which isn't to say there's anything necessarily wrong with such pursuits. Women and middle-class Colombians also play the game, although they tend to eschew booze as a performance enhancer. There are also national *tejo* tournaments, overseen by the Tejo Olympic Committee, where players are encouraged to leave behind any preconception that the sport is corrupting by nature. As the sport's official guidelines point out, '*Tejo* is an exercise of physically, socially and morally healthy goals, and not a pretext to unleash passions, rivalries, hatreds or physical or moral disorder.'

Just when the explosive element entered the game is unknown[1] but it's believed *tejo* originated as a game of the Zipa and Zaque indigenous tribes, who called it *turmequé*. Played with stones, the game was more about throwing for distance than accuracy. About 500 years ago the Spaniards

----

1 Some suspect it was between the late 1940s and late 1950s, during the era known as *La Violencia*, a tumultuous decade of political unrest in Colombia during which more than 200,000 Colombians were killed.

arrived in Colombia and adapted *turmequé*, substituting lead discs for the stone markers and making the game more about precision than strength.

In 2000, the Congress of the Republic declared *tejo* a national sport of Colombia, a decision, one might guess, greeted by the staccato of tiny explosives from the mountains to the sea.

Another tossing game

HORSESHOES

Horseshoes is an outdoor game in which competitors toss horseshoes, or horseshoe-shaped metal bars, at a stake in the ground. Played between two people, or two teams of two people each, horseshoes is usually played on grass or dirt between two stakes set 40 feet apart. Players toss their horseshoes to one stake before gathering them up and tossing them back. This process continues until a winner emerges—usually when one player has forty points (although that amount may vary at the discretion of the players and/or tournament). Points are scored in a variety of ways. When a horseshoe completely encircles the stake (without touching when it comes to rest) it is called a ringer and is worth three points. A leaner, when the horseshoe literally leans on the stake, is worth one point, sometimes two. Otherwise scoring comes down to closest to the stake. That is, the nearest horseshoe to the stake within 6 inches scores one point. If both of one player's horseshoes are closer than an opponent's within 6 inches, the former scores two points.

TOWER running

Swearing by the motto 'Use the stairs, not the elevator', tower runners belong to a subset of athletes who compete in races up tall buildings. Unlike joggers, whose uphill slogs are often rewarded with long downward sweeps of road, tower runners, in competition at least, never run anywhere but up—which means step after step after suspected collapsed lung.

It's impossible to say when humans first started racing each other up buildings but it's safe to assume it happened after the invention of stairs—which, if various pyramids are any indication, happened a long, long time before Gatorade was invented. But while the sport's origins are unclear, tower running boomed with the invention of the skyscraper and today there are dozens of vertical races around the world.[1]

---

1 Stair running does not necessarily require a building, as the punishing Niesen Stair Race demonstrates annually. Believed to be the longest continuous

While the sport has no governing body, meaning each race runs its own show, a few rules are common, the main one being that competitors tend to set off in a staggered start in order to prevent congestion in what are usually narrow stairwells without natural light and air conditioning. This may rob many of the excitement of a neck-and-neck dash to the finish line, but it reduces the risk of obstruction and injury, particularly in the early stages of a race, before the field has a chance to thin out. Having said that, some races, like the Empire State Building Run-Up, send competitors off in groups, so jostling for position is common.

Exponents of the sport like to describe tower running as a total body workout since runners are allowed to use handrails in their ascent (some stairwells, like those in the Empire State Building, are narrow enough for competitors to grasp hand rails in each hand as they climb). But the quadriceps and calves take the most punishment. Indeed, stair climbing is considerably more taxing than running, burning, by one estimation, twice as many calories in the same amount of time. For this reason tactics demand competitors pace themselves. As in most forms of racing, setting off too fast and too early leads to premature burnout.

---

staircase in the world, the Niesen staircase (usually not open to the public) is set beside the rails of a funicular rail line, which takes tourists to the top of Mount Niesen, a peak in Switzerland's Bernese Oberland range. The race is held on the narrow metal stairway and runners must negotiate a mind-boggling 11,674 stairs, taking them from an altitude of 693 metres to 2336 metres. The best climbers take just over an hour to complete the race.

The most stairs in a race, however, are the 39,700 that competitors must negotiate during the so-called Mount Everest Treppen-marathon in Radebeul, Germany. The 84.4-kilometre race is held up and down the Spitz-House staircase (which is situated between two vineyards) and requires competitors to go up and down a flight of stairs 100 times. By doing so they climb to a (virtual) altitude of 8,848 metres, the height of Mount Everest. The elite runners take at least 15 hours to finish and, one presumes, a few years to recover.

Although they've picked a gruelling sport in which to compete, tower runners—who tend to boast thighs the size of young pit bull terriers—can be consoled by the fact that when their apartment or work elevators eventually go on the blink, they will find the climb a doddle.

Top ten tower running races

1. Sears Tower, Chicago, United States, 2109 stairs

2. Menara Tower, Kuala Lumpur, Malaysia, 2058 stairs

3. Taipei 101, Taipei, Taiwan, 2046 stairs

4. CN Tower, Toronto, Canada, 1776 stairs

5. Aon Center, Chicago, United States, 1643 stairs

6. Hancock Tower, Chicago, United States, 1632 stairs

7. Empire State Building, New York City, United States, 1576 stairs

8. Sydney Tower, Sydney, Australia, 1504 stairs

9. US Bank Tower, Los Angeles, United States, 1500 stairs

10. Swissôtel, Singapore, 1336 stairs

The above order does not necessarily rank the buildings or structures in order of height —just by the number of stairs climbed by tower runners in each of the structures' respective annual races.

Ultimate (Frisbee)

Many people will recall a Frisbee as the plastic, saucer-shaped flying disc they once threw about in the 1960s and 1970s, which now resides somewhere in their garage buried under household rubble like old bicycles, kitchen appliances that seemed a good idea at the time, and bottomless boxes full of broken hearts and shattered dreams.

Not everyone, however, saw the flying disc as a passing fad and during the late 1960s and early 1970s American college students began using the disc as a glorified—and aerodynamically glorious—ball in a team game resembling netball, Australian Rules football and, because catching the disc within end-zones is the means of scoring, American football. The non-contact game came to be known as Ultimate Frisbee, although today the 'Frisbee' has been dropped, as it is a brand name of a particular type of flying disc not necessarily used to play the game.

Ultimate is played in both pick-up and organized forms, the former referring to casual games made up of a random number of like-minded people who get together in a park using cones or items of clothing as boundary markers. In its organized form Ultimate is a game of halves played between two teams of seven players (substitutions are allowed) on a field measuring 64 metres by 37 metres, not including two 18-metre-deep end zones. The game is widely played in the United States in high schools and colleges, and it is similarly popular among student bodies in many European countries, as well as Canada, Australia and New Zealand. Each country has its own governing body and the World Flying Disc Federation oversees many international tournaments.

Ultimate starts with both teams lined up along the front line of their respective end zones, with one team throwing, or 'pulling', the 175-gram disc to the opposition. The aim of the game is to outscore the other team with a point awarded for catching a disc within the opposition's end zone. Usually Ultimate games are played to a pre-determined number of points (generally seventeen), in order to stop a team running down the clock when they have a lead; a cynical tactic employed in many other sports, such as football (soccer).

Another distinctive rule is that while players can move anywhere within the field, and throw in any direction they like, they must come to a stop soon after catching a disc (a few steps are permitted since stopping dead during a full run is nigh on impossible). This is similar to netball where players are not allowed to take more than one step after catching a ball. Should they travel with the disc, or fail to pass it within 10 seconds of receiving it, a violation has occurred and the defensive team gets possession of the disc. Change of possession also occurs when the offensive team throws the disc to the ground or out-of-bounds; when an offensive player drops the disc; and when a defender catches the disc, or knocks it out of the air and on to the ground.

Interestingly, and uniquely, Ultimate games have no official referee, even during competitions and tournaments. Such self-regulation appears to be a nod to Frisbee's origins as a representation of the laid-back, free-spirited lifestyle prominent at the time; the kind of thing a certain bell-bottom-wearing type might have partaken of in a park while he was in an LSD haze or enjoying a post-coital high which, to play on stereotypes that employ rose-coloured glasses, occurred every 26 minutes or so. (Of course, kids would have played with Frisbees too, not just hippies, and no one's suggesting they used LSD or had sex as frequently as every 26 minutes. For one thing, they were in school.)

Ironically, however, it could be argued that playing Ultimate—or using a flying disc in a regimented athletic format with rules, points, winners and losers—might seem to be a corruption of an ideal. Then again, while this is what hippies may have thought when they were first tossing the disc around parks, they are now bald, wearing suits and negative-gearing their properties, so they probably don't care any more.

Whether Ultimate is or isn't a corruption of the Frisbee spirit is, to its fans, a moot point. They are too busy having fun, not to mention trying to get a handle on the art of throwing a disc. After all, mastery of a flying disc is no easy thing, as anyone who has ever tried to throw a disc to a friend and ended up seeing it twist violently in the air, land on its end and roll into the next suburb will know (such a throw would be described, in Ultimate parlance, as swill[1]). The best Ultimate players, however, are not only athletic and able to catch the

---

1 Perhaps because it's played by students, who have always enjoyed a good colloquialism, Ultimate employs numerous jargon terms including:

    Bid—an impressive (but failing) diving attempt to catch the disc.

    Greatest—a highlight-reel manoeuvre in which a player jumps from inside the field of play and over the boundary line but, while still in the air, catches the disc and redirects it back into the field of play and into the hands of a team-mate. The greatest 'greatest' would occur if the redirected throw was caught in the end zone for a point.

disc in mid-air while leaping over an opponent or diving at full stretch, but they can influence the speed and path of a thrown disc by using a variety of different grips and throwing techniques.

Despite the difficulties of controlling the disc, novices should not be afraid to play the game. Just don't set up your field amid a lot of tall trees. Not unless you have a ladder on hand.

Huck—a long, powerful pull (also known as a 'bomb') that travels a great distance.

Layout—a dive to catch the disc.

Pull—a long throw that initiates the start of play, similar to a kickoff in many forms of football.

Sky—leaping and catching the disc at an impressive—and most satisfying—height over a forlorn opponent, who might consider herself 'skied'. Such jumping contests resemble 'marking' contests in Australian Rules football where a number of players look to out-leap each other to be the first to grab a football that has been kicked.

Spike—similar to what American footballers do when they score a touchdown, a spike is when a player throws the disc down onto the ground in celebration after scoring. Many Ultimate players frown upon the spike since it reeks of showboating and may warp the disc.

Swill—a bad throw.

Taco—a disc that has become warped due to a foot block, a player stepping on it, or a throw that nosedives into the ground. Generally a 'taco-ed' disc is either straightened by the next handler or is removed from play and repaired on the sideline.

Universe Point—when each team only needs one more point to win the game, the point is called a universe point.

Some other games using a flying disc

DISC GOLF

As its name suggests, disc golf is a game that largely follows the objectives and rules of golf except that instead of hitting a small ball with a club into a number of holes, players throw a flying disc, aiming at either natural or specially designed targets.

Similar to a golf course, a disc golf course (normally a park, although there are more than 1000 permanent disc-golf courses in the world, most of them in the United States) consists of eighteen holes, or targets, which can be natural objects such as trees or, on a prepared course, metal baskets, above which hang a number of small chains. The disc golfer doesn't so much have to land the disc directly into the basket, which sits about 1 metre off the ground, but can hit the chains, which rob the disc of its momentum, causing it to drop like a shot duck into the basket below.

Like golf, each hole is given a par rating; par being the number of shots (throws) a good player would commonly need to complete the hole. The total length of the average hole is about 100 metres.

It's believed disc golf was invented around the same time as Ultimate and the first disc-golf course was opened in 1975 in Los Angeles County, California. Today there are even disc-golf professionals playing a number of tournaments in the United States, winning prizes in the order of US$40,000.

DODGE (FRISBEE)

Dodge (Frisbee) is similar to dodge ball except it uses a flying disc instead of a ball. The game is played on a small court about the size of a basketball court. Two teams occupy the space on their own side of the halfway line. The team that starts with the disc throws it hard towards the opposition with the intention of hitting someone. If they are successful the person struck must leave the court. If, however, the intended target catches the disc, before or after it hits her, the thrower leaves the court. The catcher then becomes the thrower. There may be more than one disc in play at any one time. One team wins when all the opposition players have been hit and have left the court.

FREESTYLE

What ice dancing is to speed skating, freestyle is to Ultimate. That is to say, it is based in athletics but driven by aesthetics and acrobatics. In essence, freestyle exponents, competing in teams of two, throw a flying disc back and forth with the intention of catching the disc in as spectacular a way as possible (the behind the back catch is child's play to a seasoned freestyler, who can all but make a disc fetch his pipe and slippers). The catch and throw game is not left to chance or improvization, at least for competitions. Pairs choreograph routines (often to music) they believe will catch the judges' eyes. Routines are 3–5 minutes in length, with scores out of ten awarded for the difficulty, artistic impression and execution of the routine, giving a total score out of thirty.

Since a marathon is a footrace measuring precisely 42.195 kilometres[1], an ultramarathon is any race longer than that. Which is to say, too long.

Ultramarathon races take place anywhere in the world where people are silly enough to push their bodies so hard that muscle meltdown, death and, even worse, public bowel failure are possible side-effects. Compared to these, blisters the size of Belgium are not even worth mentioning, apart from this once.

---

1 A marathon references a legendary run from Marathon to Athens made by a Greek soldier in 490 BC. In one version of the tale, the soldier, believed to be named Pheidippides, ran the 26-mile distance to break the news to the Athenians that the Persians had been defeated in battle. Legend has it that he delivered his news and promptly dropped dead—becoming the first but certainly not the last person to seek such relief after running the kind of distance one should only contemplate covering in an automobile.

Ultramarathon races, which have been run ever since people felt a need to explore their potential and test themselves, either take place over set distances or set times, meaning in the latter case that the winner will be the person who covers the most distance within the time limit. In terms of venue, ultramarathon races take place on standard athletics tracks, dirt roads, highways, mountain passes and even deserts.

The International Association of Ultrarunners—which is sanctioned by the world athletic body, the International Association of Athletics Federations (IAAF)—holds annual world championships for several distances and times including 50 kilometres, 100 kilometres and 24 hours. But races run by other organizations can last several days and be run over extraordinary distances, such as the so-called Self-Transcendence 3100-Mile Race (see page 238). By comparison, Australia's now defunct Sydney to Melbourne Ultra Marathon, an 875-kilometre footrace once famously won by 61-year-old potato and dairy farmer Cliff Young, was a mere stroll.[2]

Like other endurance athletes, ultramarathon runners are battling themselves as much as the opposition. It's said that after running about 30 kilometres the body has used up its glycogen stores and other forms of energy. It then

---

At the first Olympic Games in Athens in 1896 a race was held over the same distance (26 miles) to commemorate Pheidippides' run. At the 1908 London Olympics, however, Queen Alexandra, consort to Edward VII, suggested the race be lengthened by 385 yards so that it started on the grounds of Windsor Castle, meaning she and her children would barely have to get out of their pyjamas and night tiaras to see the athletes set off.

In 1924, 26 miles 385 yards (42.195 km) became the standard distance for the marathon.

2 Young averaged between 8 and 9 minutes per kilometre, considerably slower than most of his competitors. But Young, famous for running around his farm in gumboots, and a running style closer to shuffling than striding, barely rested. In 1983, the year of his victory in 5 days, 15 hours and 4 minutes, Young ran the first 2 days without significant sleep, catching his younger competitors off guard.

begins, in a sense, to eat itself. While an ultramarathon runner is of course allowed to eat, drink and sleep (although he'd be mad slipping away for a kip in a 50-kilometre race because, by the time he woke up asking the nearest person 'What time is it?' the race would be long over), his body has to withstand tremendous stress. His mind also faces a stern test as he attempts to shut out the pain and suffering he is enduring, not to mention negative thoughts and unhelpful questions such as, 'What was I thinking?', 'Am I just doing this to make myself feel better about myself?' and 'What's that *smell?*'[3]

Some significant ultramarathon races

THE MARATHON DES SABLES

Considered one of the world's toughest foot races, the Marathon des Sables, or marathon of the sands, is an annual 6-day, 243-kilometre ultramarathon through the Sahara Desert in southern Morocco. Other races may be longer but the Marathon des Sables tests competitors with its searing day heat

---

3 On the bright side, ultramarathoners do not have to worry about being shot, which was the premise of a 1979 Stephen King novella, *The Long Walk*. Writing under the pseudonym Richard Bachman, King plotted a most interesting athletic event—particularly for spectators—called the Long Walk, which was an ultramarathon event with no finish line, time limit or designated rest stops. The winner was simply the last person left alive, for if any competitor ever fell behind a constant speed of 4 miles per hour he would receive a warning. If he received a third warning, soldiers monitoring the race would shoot the athlete dead.

(averaging 30–48 degrees Celsius), cold nights (4–14 degrees Celsius), possible sandstorms and an undulating course over rocky ground and soft desert sand, which is said to chafe like sandpaper. Compounding things, competitors must carry anything they plan to eat and drink on their person (race organizers distribute a minimum 9 litres per day per person), as well as a sleeping bag. Organizers only supply tents, setting them up at the end of each day's stage; stages vary in length from 22 kilometres to 82 kilometres. Competitors can at least get regular sleep, as they start each day with the kilometre count and time they finished with the previous evening.

Without a doubt the race's star is Moroccan Lahcen Ahansal who, up to and including 2007, has won the race ten times.

THE SELF-TRANSCENDENCE 3100-MILE RACE

As 3100 miles converts to 4989 kilometres, it seems safe to assume that the unusual name of this race is a nice way of saying that competitors are so destroyed by its demands that they effectively leave their body or, to put it another way, lose their minds.

Believed to be the longest footrace in the world, this test of endurance and survival—held at Flushing Meadows Park, New York City—has a 51-day time limit during which athletes attempt to complete 5649 laps of a course measuring 0.5448 miles. This means competitors must average just over 60 miles per day to stay on pace. Many have successfully done so.

Curiously, the race used to be 2700 miles over 47 days, but race founder, endurance athlete and spiritualist Sri Chinmoy, upped the distance in 1997. Come to think of it, 2700 miles did seem a little easy.

THE CLIFF YOUNG AUSTRALIAN SIX-DAY RACE

The Australian Six-Day Race has been held most years since 1984 on a 400-metre dirt circuit at the Memorial Square in the centre of Colac, Victoria. The winner is the person who runs the greatest distance in the six days. In 2005, 49-year-old Greek distance runner Yiannis Kouros set a world six-day track record when he clocked up 1036.85 kilometres, sleeping a total of 3 hours. Kouros had won the event 21 years earlier when he set a then six-day track record of 1023.2 kilometres.

THE BADWATER ULTRAMARATHON

Proclaiming itself the world's 'most demanding' race, this insane 135-mile odyssey starts at 280 feet below sea level at Badwater Basin in California's aptly named Death Valley where, in July, when the race is held, temperatures can get close to 130 degrees Fahrenheit. The race finishes only 80 miles away (as the crow flies at least) at the Mount Whitney Portals, an elevation of 8360 feet. With competitors having to cross three mountain ranges they end up, cumulatively, climbing 13,000 feet and descending 4700 feet.

The race has been held since 1977 and the course record is 24 hours, 36 minutes and 8 seconds, set by American Scott Jurek in 2005. The best women's time is 27 hours, 56 minutes and 47 seconds set by American Pam Reed in 2002.

THE LAST DESERT

Held in Antarctica, a continent better known for penguins and explorers with blackened noses and missing digits, The Last Desert is a 250-kilometre invitation-only ultramarathon for competitors who have proven themselves in the three other 250-kilometre desert races that make up what's known as the Four Deserts series: The Gobi March (China), The Atacama Crossing (Chile), and The Sahara Race (Egypt).

Depending on the weather, which can change faster than Madonna during a live show, stages can vary from 16–160 kilometres. And unlike in the other Four Deserts events, where competitors must carry their own provisions, runners are fed and put up every night on an Antarctic research vessel. While the runners are sleeping and dreaming of sun-kissed tropical beaches, the ship sails to a new stage location chosen for its differing terrain. Cut-off times are established daily so that anyone walking the course can complete it.

UnderWater hockey

To an outsider familiar with the density of water, playing ball games while submerged in the stuff seems as pointless as holding a regatta in a desert, or a game of badminton in a cyclone.

That said, since its invention in 1954,[1] underwater hockey has grown into an international sport with a bi-annual world championship event. So unless all the participants are simply playing to prove a point (that ball sports can be played underwater and, dammit, they're fun too) there must be something to it—not that it will ever be obvious to spectators who, unless they don a

---

1 Underwater hockey was invented in 1954 in order to give members of a British dive team something to do during the months when the North Sea was just too cold to explore (which you'd think would be 12 months of the year, but there you go). At the time, it was devised as a game for eight-person teams and since promoting the puck with the stick is known as a push, the alternative name of octopush makes some sense.

swimsuit and goggles, might as well be leaning over the edge of a boat watching mackerel mating.

With some similarities to ice hockey and field hockey, underwater hockey, also known as octopush, is a non-contact sport played between two teams. Each spend their time trying to defy water resistance by attempting to propel a small, weighted puck into their opponent's goal by hitting it along the pool bottom with 30-centimetre long sticks, sometimes known as bats. Though equipped with a mask, fins and a snorkel (not to mention a mouthguard, gloves and a water polo-style cap as added safety measures), underwater hockey players do not carry artificial breathing apparatus, which means they must constantly resurface to breathe. For this reason teamwork and well-timed substitutions are particularly important in both attack and defence, as no one wants to waste, or allow, a golden scoring opportunity on account of their drowning.

To adhere to the rules of the sport's governing body, the Confédération Mondiale des Activités Subaquatiques (also known, in English, as the World Underwater Federation, which sounds nowhere near as impressive), underwater hockey must be played in a pool 21–25 metres long, 12–15 metres wide and about 2 metres deep. Each goal is 3 metres long and is situated midway along each of the two end lines. The game runs for 10–15 minute halves, and there are ten players in each side with no more than six players from each team in the water at any one time. Substitutions may occur continually.

Play starts with the 1.3–1.5-kilogram plastic-coated lead puck placed in the centre of the pool. Teams are lined up above their respective goals and on the referee's call play commences, usually with the two fastest swimmers on each team racing each other to get first possession of the puck. Once the puck is in a team's possession they will attempt to work the puck between them (obviously long, raking passes are out of the question) in their search for a goal. In both attack and defence only the player's stick may be used to propel or stop the puck and any attempt to block an opponent's access to the puck is viewed by the referees (there are two in the water, using scuba gear, and at least one on deck) as a foul and will be penalized accordingly. Repeated and/or dangerous fouls may see a player ejected from play.

Other underwater ball sports

UNDERWATER RUGBY

Another lung-busting sport that tests the durability of one's swimming-costume elastic, underwater rugby is a contact sport in which the object of the game is to score a goal by throwing a grapefruit-sized weighted ball (it is slightly negatively buoyed, meaning it will sink, but slowly) into an opponent's goal—represented by a metal bucket with a 40-centimetre diameter, which sits on the bottom of the 3.5–5-metre-deep pool. The six players on each team (with five substitutes each) pass the ball backwards and forwards between them in attempting to score. Tackling opponents with the ball is allowed. The ball must remain underwater at all times, and substitutions, as in underwater hockey, are continual. As with underwater hockey, players are kitted out in snorkelling gear—fins, masks and snorkels.

Ludwig von Bersuda, a member of the Cologne-based German Underwater Club, created underwater rugby in the 1960s. Today the game is most popular in Europe. The game's resemblance to actual rugby is negligible. 'Underwater water polo' would better describe the game.

UNDERWATER FOOTBALL

Almost identical to underwater rugby is underwater football—a game that differs mainly in how points are scored. Instead of using underwater rugby's weighted bucket, a goal in underwater football is scored when an attacking player forces the ball onto a section of gutter on the pool end his team is attacking. In this it most resembles a 'try' in rugby. Blocking an attacking player is allowed, as is stripping—stripping the player of the ball, that is, not the player of his clothes. It is also an offence for a player to carry the ball within his swimming costume, no matter whom he is trying to impress.

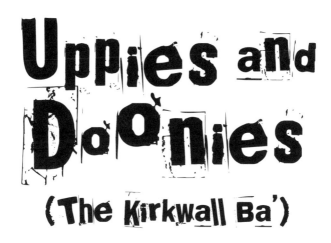

Uppies and Doonies

(The Kirkwall Ba')

Speckled over the North Sea off the wind-ravaged tip of Scotland, the Orkney Islands are a verdant (if chilly) haven from the din of big-city living; there are open spaces, green fields, stone walls, widescreen skies and the kind of white-tipped, wild-ocean views that make you think of woolly jumpers, wheeling gulls and grief-stricken widows who spend all their time staring out of salt-encrusted windows, waiting for someone who's just not coming back on account of that fishing boat swallowed by the sea during the great storm of '92. Lest one gets overly contemplative, however, the Orkney Islands are also home to an ancient football game called the Ba', which has no rules, hundreds of players on each side and a playing field that is actually the entire town of Kirkwall. Organized mayhem is a fitting description.

An example of the kind of centuries-old, mob-football games still played in various parts of the United Kingdom (see page 248), the Kirkwall Ba', which has records stretching back 150 years or so, is played twice a year and is a contest between two sections of the town's male residents. The sections are determined by birth: those born north of St Magnus Cathedral, called Doonies (in that they were born Doon-the-Gates), and those born south of the Cathedral, Uppies (Up-the-Gates)[1].

The game-cum-civil war's centrepiece is the Ba', a handmade leather ball filled with cork. Every Christmas Day and New Year's Day competitors assemble in their hundreds (there are no limits) on Broad Street in the centre of Kirkwall. When the cathedral clock strikes 1 pm[2] the Ba' is tossed from the Mercat Cross in front of St Magnus' into the middle of the pack of competitors and the game is on. There are no set rules other than how the game is won: the Doonies have to toss the ball into the waters of Kirkwall Bay, while the Uppies have to touch the Ba' onto the wall at Sandison's Corner. Both the bay, to the north, and Sandison's Corner, to the south, are approximately 500 metres in a straight line from the cathedral, although the Ba's journey will be through a dogleg of streets and flagstone lanes along which prudent shopkeepers have boarded up their windows. Possible obstacles, such as small children, the elderly and expensive motor vehicles, should have long made themselves scarce. It's doubtful that a rolling, roiling mob has the presence of mind to 'keep off the flowers', as it were.

---

1 Gates seems to be a corruption of *gata*, which is Old Norse for 'path' or 'road'. Of course, these days, the residents of Kirkwall are generally born in a hospital, so family loyalties tend to determine which side you're on.

2 As well as the men's game commencing at 1 pm, there is also a game for the town's boys that starts at 10.30 am. As for women, well, no one is stopping them joining in but it's a rare, though hardly surprising occurrence, given the bulk of the male players who appear to have eaten nothing but metal shavings from the moment of their birth, as if in readiness for Ba' games.

   On Christmas Day 1945 and New Year's Day 1946, Ba' games for female competitors were held for the first and only times to date. It seems the town's menfolk didn't feel the bruising and sometimes violent nature of the game was suitable. They had no compunction letting their young boys play it, however.

Due to the throng outside the cathedral, a Ba' swallowed by the crowd isn't disgorged easily. A mass scrum forms around it with the vast majority of players never sighting it, let alone touching it. Like the tide, this scrum ebbs and flows as Doonies and Uppies push against each other, both groups trying to edge the Ba' into a street or lane, which may hasten victory. Should the scrum reach Junction Road a breakaway is always possible due to the width of the thoroughfare. But in the narrow lanes of Kirkwall the scrum—which steams in the winter air like a cracked-open baked potato fresh from the oven—can get bogged down for hours. And men being men, some competitors, on occasion, don't feel pushing is enough and the odd punch is thrown to help clear a path, alleviate pent up tension, settle a score and, possibly, for the pure fun of it.[3] Most injuries, however, occur not from blows but from the heaving crush of bodies (fainting is reasonably common) or from getting mashed against an unforgiving wall.

Uppies and Doonies is seemingly a game where weight of numbers is everything but tactics and good organizing also play a role in victory. Combatants sometimes wheel away from a scrum pretending they have the Ba' in order to attract opponents and give the actual Ba'-holder room to move. Rooftops have sometimes been used by nimble locals to steal the Ba' away from the masses. Also, astute players on the fringes of the scrum beckon their

----

3 'It breaks out twice a year at a time when peace and goodwill might be expected to prevail, the warring armies engaging in close combat with a ferocity that precludes respect for person or property. Even the law has been known to stand impotent as combatants surged and counter-surged through the environs of the police station, and memory has hardly dimmed the occasion when the local manse was invaded and despoiled. Casualties are high—but who cares? Crushed ribs and broken limbs are never enough reasons for the enthusiastic participants to desist from this traditional orgy of Orcadian violence which not even a sheriff's edict could ban—the Kirkwall Ba' Game.'
    —*Spectrum*, BBC Television, 1982

charges to certain spots in order to strengthen a promising push or reinforce a possible breach.

Positioning players away from the scrum in case a breakaway is possible is also prudent. In 2006, a Doonie emerged from the scrum with the Ba' in his hand, tossed it over a wall into the hands of a loitering fellow Doonie and the fellow high-tailed it to the bay, securing the first Ba' victory for the Doonies in sixteen attempts.

Finally, when the game is won, the actual Ba' is awarded to a player from the winning team who is thought to have played a major role in the victory, or someone who has been a notable participant over the years. As an extra, though somewhat dubious, honour, everyone goes around to his place for a drink.

Other mob football games

ASHBOURNE, DERBYSHIRE, UNITED KINGDOM

The Royal Shrovetide Football match, played every Shrove Tuesday and Ash Wednesday, can trace its roots to the twelfth century. Legend has it that the earliest form of the game used a severed head, which had been tossed into the crowd following an execution. This, you must remember, was in the days before television, when a severed head tossed your way was something to be enjoyed.

Like the Kirkwall Ba', the Ashbourne game is a minimally structured contest[4] in which a ball is tossed into a crowd and two large teams attempt to progress it through the centre of town to their respective goals. In this case, the two teams are known as the Up'ards (those born north of the River Henmore, which divides the Georgian market town) and Down'ards. There are two river-side goalposts 3 miles apart; one at what was once Sturston Mill, where the Up'ards attempt to score, and one at the former Clifton Mill, where the Down'ards attempt to score. A player must be in the water when goaling (or scoring), which requires hitting the ball against the millstones three successive times.

After a pre-game luncheon at the Green Man Royal Hotel (during which the game's anthem, 'Tis a glorious game, deny it who can, That tries the pluck of an Englishman' is sung), the assembled crowd gathers around a historic plinth in the town centre—a plinth that now happens to be in the car park of a shopping centre. They then sing 'Auld Lang Syne' and 'God Save the Queen' before the match commences at 2 pm when the ball is tossed in the air, or 'turned up'. With the ball now in play, the Up'ards and Down'ards form what the locals call a 'hug'. Anyone else might call it a riot in slow motion. If the ball

4 The rules of the game include:
   • Committing murder or manslaughter is prohibited. Unnecessary violence is frowned upon.
   • The ball may not be carried in a motorized vehicle.
   • The ball may not be hidden in a bag, coat or rucksack etc.
   • Cemeteries, churchyards and the town memorial gardens are strictly out of bounds.
   • Playing after 10 pm is forbidden.

----

is goaled before 5 pm play restarts from the town centre. No matter what, play ends for the day at 10 pm.

WORKINGTON, CUMBRIA, UNITED KINGDOM

Held every Easter to raise money for local charities, Workington's Uppies and Downies event is a three-game series featuring goals a mile apart; the Downies' goal a capstan at the harbour, the Uppies' the gates of Workington Hall. Upon reaching the goal a player must complete the formalities and 'hail' the ball, by raising it over his head three times (the person who hails the ball may not necessarily be the one who brought it to the goal). With no time limits or rules, it's a swarming mess of a game and is responsible for at least one death, that of 20-year-old Robert Storey who drowned in the River Derwent in 1983 while swimming towards the harbour with three other Downies, one of whom had the ball. As with other traditional football games, female players are very rare. No woman had ever hailed the ball—until 2006, that is, when 29-year-old Catherine Malloy became the first woman to score a goal when she won the series for the Uppies at the third and final match.

JEDBURGH, SCOTLAND

In the Jedburgh ba' game of Uppies and Downies, the Uppies score by hailing the softball-sized leather ball (a 'handba', said to represent the head of an English prisoner-of-war—it would contravene the Geneva convention today, but it's a re-enactment of medieval times) at the Jedburgh Castle wall, the Downies by hailing it at the Jedwater river.

Wife Carrying

Good-humouredly inspired by times long gone when antsy warriors were known to raid a neighbour's village with the sole intent of making off with another man's good lady without so much as a 'So what's your star sign?', wife carrying is a festival-style sport contested in a number of countries around the world.

This sport, which is unlikely to ever be sponsored by a feminist organization, was introduced in Sonkajärvi, Finland, in 1992 when the inaugural Wife Carrying World Championships were held. First a race over snow-packed hill and dale, the championships are now held on a specially designed 253.5-metre sand, grass and gravel track littered with obstacles, such as log hurdles and a 1-metre-deep water hazard. These days there is also a separate competition for sprinters over a 100-metre course and a teams relay event where a 'wife' is used as a kind of baton between three men who each run a third of the course before handing her over.

As the name of the sport makes clear, male competitors have to do most of the work. Yet before the heavy lifting begins, their first task is to find a wife to carry. Though the first prize is the wife's weight in beer it is, arguably, not a good enough reason for single men to get hitched. Fortunately, the rules allow the competitor to carry anyone's wife, as long as she is over seventeen years old, more than 49 kilograms and freely gives her consent.[1]

With 49 kilograms the cut-off weight, it is obviously in a male competitor's best interests to find a wife as close to that mark as possible. While he will earn considerable kudos for lugging around a woman large enough to feature on reality TV programs such as *The Biggest Loser*, he is unlikely to win. Should he happen to do so, however, he will be able to get drunk for the best part of a year without spending a cent.

The championships, held in July, do not dictate what carrying style a man should use. Some use the fireman's lift (where the wife is draped sideways across the man's shoulders with one arm and leg hanging down over his chest, providing him with convenient 'handles'), some the piggyback. One other popular hold is Estonian-style, in which the wife hangs face-in, upside down with her legs hanging over the man's shoulder, her arms wrapped around his torso and her face disturbingly close to his backside. Should you be carrying a woman using such a style, bear in mind that her head may be submerged in the water hazards. So be quick. Also bear in mind that should you drop your wife you will be penalized 15 seconds. Chances are you may also have to find your own way home.

Finland's Wife Carrying World Championships are conducted through a series of heats but the winner is the couple who complete the course the fastest.

---

1 If a wife's weight is less than 49 kilograms she must wear a rucksack weighted to bring her up to that mark.

Estonians have thus far dominated the championships. Estonian couples have won all the past nine titles with Margo Uusorg the most dominant male, having won numerous titles and set the standing record of 55.5 seconds.[2]

Since Finland made this curious contribution to world sport and culture, wife-carrying competitions are now held in a number of countries around the world, including the United States (the North American Wife Carrying Championships take place every year on Columbus Day Weekend in October at Sunday River Ski Resort in Newry, Maine) and Australia (the Australian Wife Carrying Titles are held in the Hunter Valley, New South Wales, every March). Both tournaments include in their prize an invitation to compete in the world championships in Finland.

----

2 Happily married men out with their wives must get worried when Estonian Margo
   Uusorg hoves into view knowing, as they do, that the Estonian could snatch up
   their wives and run off with them at a challenging gallop. Unhappily married
   men, on the other hand, may start to think things are looking up.

Conversion tables

To convert metric measurements to or from Imperial, multiply the number of units by the following factors:

LENGTH

FROM	TO	MULTIPLY BY
centimetres	inches	0.3937
feet	metres	0.3048
inches	metres	0.0254
inches	centimetres	2.54
metres	yards	1.0936
metres	feet	3.2808
metres	inches	39.37
yards	metres	0.9144

MASS

FROM	TO	MULTIPLY BY
kilograms	pounds	2.2046
pounds	kilograms	0.4536
stone	kilograms	6.3502

TEMPERATURE

FROM	TO	MULTIPLY BY
Celsius (degrees C)	Fahrenheit (degrees F)	9/5 x C + 32
Fahrenheit (degrees F)	Celsius (degrees C)	5/9 x (temperature − 32)

VELOCITY AND SPEED

FROM	TO	MULTIPLY BY
kilometres per hour	miles per hour	0.6214
miles per hour	kilometres per hour	1.6093

VOLUME

FROM	TO	MULTIPLY BY
gallons (UK)	litres	4.54609
gallons (US)	litres	3.7854
litres	gallons (UK)	0.22

Acknowledgments

Working on the premise that I'm willing to share the credit if they're willing to share the blame, much thanks to the team at Murdoch Books Australia for their efforts in getting this book into print and onto the shelves. Special thanks to my two editors, Rhiain Hull and Janine Flew, whose raised eyebrows and necessary pedantry saved me from a few blushes and made the book a better product. Thanks too to Jacqui Smith for her administrative efforts. And I'm particularly grateful to commissioning editor, Hazel Flynn. Not only for choosing me (I believe by throwing a dart at a list of prospective authors), but also, after tossing me the bare bones of an idea, being happy to stand back and let me flesh it out as I saw fit. While my friends and family could certainly have supplied me with a few more ideas, they were at least supportive. So cheers, Niall, Kieran, Ann-Siobhan, Mum and Dad (who, above all, has taught me that sport can be both wonderful and worthwhile yet never worth crying or fighting over). And, finally, on the home front I couldn't have managed at all without my wonderful partner Lee who, though she'd given birth to our dearest Abbie before I'd even cobbled together a possible contents list, allowed me to skip my fair share of sleepless nights and dirty nappies. Greater love hath no woman than this.

CREDITS
Page 19: Ten Canmandments © Darwin Beer Can Regatta, Lions Club of Darwin, www.beercanregatta.org.au. Used with permission. **Page 34:** Quote reproduced with permission of Bossaball SL. **Page 172:** Quote reproduced with the permission of the Pillow Fighting League. **Page 174:** Extract from Race Walking regulations used with permission of International Association of Athletic Federations (IAAF). **Pages 186–187:** Gambits from the World RPS Society's website reproduced with permission. **Pages 215–216:** Tchoukball charter reproduced with permission.

First published in 2007 by Pier 9, an imprint of Murdoch Books Pty Limited

Murdoch Books Australia
Pier 8/9
23 Hickson Road
Millers Point NSW 2000
Phone: +61 (0) 2 8220 2000
Fax: +61 (0) 2 8220 2558
www.murdochbooks.com.au

Murdoch Books UK Limited
Erico House, 6th Floor
93–99 Upper Richmond Road
Putney, London SW15 2TG
Phone: +44 (0) 20 8785 5995
Fax: +44 (0) 20 8785 5985
www.murdochbooks.co.uk

Chief Executive: Juliet Rogers
Publishing Director: Kay Scarlett

Commissioning Editor: Hazel Flynn
Concept and Design: Reuben Crossman
Project Manager and Editor: Rhiain Hull
Production: Kita George

National Library of Australia Cataloguing-in-Publication Data

Connolly, Paul, 1968– .
The world's weirdest sports: bog snorkelling, goat grabbing, dwile flonking and more...
ISBN 9781921259975 (pbk.). 1. Sports. 2. Extreme sports. I. Title. 796.046

A catalogue record for this book is available from the British Library.

Printed by iBook Printing Ltd. in 2007. PRINTED IN CHINA.